DEPARTMENT OF SOCIAL SECURITY

RESEARCH REPORT No 56

CONFIDENTIALITY: THE PUBLIC VIEW

A qualitative study

Alan Hedges

A report of research carried out by Alan Hedges, on behalf of the Department of Social Security

London: The Stationery Office

First published 1996

ISBN 0 11 762434 9

ISSN 0961 5695

Views expressed in this report are not necessarily those of the Department or any other government department.

CONTENTS

1 Overview *1*

1.1 The research *1*

1.2 Conclusions and recommendations *1*

2 The Study *12*

2.1 Objective *12*

2.2 General method *12*

2.3 Qualitative study *12*

2.3.1 Sample 13

2.3.2 Further details of method 13

2.3.3 Areas 13

2.3.4 Stimulus material 13

2.3.5 The group sessions 14

2.3.6 Responsibilities 14

2.3.7 Limitations and caveats 14

2.3.8 Timing 14

2.3.9 Verbatims 14

2.3.10 This report 15

2.3.11 Terms used 15

3 Literature Review *17*

4 Findings of the Study *19*

4.1 Personal information and confidentiality *19*

4.1.1 What is personal information (PI)? 19

4.1.2 Ownership of information 19

4.1.3 Level of awareness and concern 19

4.1.4 Trust in organisations 31

4.1.5 Attitudes to confidentiality 33

4.1.6 What does 'confidential' mean? 34

4.1.7 Why people prize confidentiality 38

4.1.8 Information technology 42

4.2 Using and disclosing PI *45*

4.2.1 Possible data relationships 45

4.2.2 Sharing and pooling information 45

4.2.3 Reliability 51

4.2.4 Safeguards and protection 54

4.2.5 Subject access 59

4.2.6 Different types of information 62

4.3 DSS *68*

4.3.1 General perceptions of DSS 68

4.3.2 DSS and personal information 70

4.3.3 Clarifying the DSS status of PI *73*
4.3.4 Scenarios *75*
4.3.5 Sharing DSS data with other bodies *90*
4.3.6 DSS policies and practices *100*
4.3.7 Effects of policy change *101*

Annexes

I Methods and sample *105*
II Sample profile *109*
III Recruitment questionnaire *110*
IV Topic guide *112*
V Stimulus material *117*
VI List of sources consulted *128*
VII Letter of authority *130*

1 OVERVIEW

1.1 The research

The purpose of the study was to explore the public's perspective on the handling and uses of personal information (PI) as input to a DSS policy review.

The research was carried out by independent researcher Alan Hedges. It is based on a set of qualitative interviews, preceded by a brief literature review. The interviews:

- were carried out in 8 small group sessions and 8 individual interviews
- involved 69 members of the adult English population (16+)
- were completed between November '95 and January '96.

The work is small in scale and designed to provide understanding of a complex topic rather than statistical evidence. The report aims to present this understanding – which, although firmly grounded in what people said, draws on the whole tone and pattern of the discussion as well as on specific comments from participants.

1.2 Conclusions and recommendations

The main findings and conclusions from the survey are summarised briefly below. I also give my recommendations for action arising from these (indented paragraphs in contrasting type, marked on the left with a vertical line). The recommendations sometimes reflect suggestions made by participants, but they are essentially my own responses to what people said. They arise purely from this general public research – I have not made any direct appraisal of DSS systems and practices, nor any economic or other evaluation of the options.

1) Concern about PI and confidentiality: I found widespread but largely unfocused public concern about the confidentiality and uses of personal information. This arises mainly from the combination of two factors:

a) a feeling that such information now circulates more widely and freely, through a combination of growing information technology and changing organisational culture

b) a sense of ignorance about what actually happens.

Participants seemed largely ignorant about what happens to their personal information – they can't observe where it goes after they hand it over, and feel they are not told how it is used and stored, where it might be passed on to, or what use is made of it. Most feel they have a right to know, since the information belongs morally to them. Trust in the organisations who hold PI usually seems limited – and may be declining. People feel entitled to expect confidentiality, but not at all sure how far they get it. They are sometimes surprised how much seems to be known about them by various bodies – which raises uncomfortable questions about how PI circulates.

Concern seems fairly strong and widespread, although more a background unease than a front line-worry – not usually so high in priority as practical issues like unemployment, combating crime or getting benefit entitlement, for example. PI concerns are usually more front-of-mind in relation to the private sector (junk mail, credit ratings etc), but sometimes seem more significant in relation to the public sector, which can have a major effect on people's lives.

Some participants seemed to exaggerate the problem in their minds (partly because they don't understand how computers and networks operate), but others may understate the scale of information transfer. Concern tends to increase as the issues are discussed. Not *knowing* is in itself disturbing.

2) Defining confidentiality in practice: 'Confidentiality' is a simple concept, but participants find it increasingly hard to know how to apply it to large, complex and increasingly interlinked organisations – at what point does disclosure start to breach confidence? However, it remains an important matter to most people for three main kinds of reason:

a) The personal information organisations hold can affect individuals' interests – perhaps without them even knowing

b) Most people have a strong sense of personal privacy which they feel is violated by circulation of PI to people who have "no business to know"

c) If organisations (including the State) have too much information about individuals it could tip the balance of power between State and citizen – which makes some people feel impotent and apprehensive.

3) Transaction-based confidentiality: Bland statements about 'confidentiality' don't help unless people can be given a sense of what this actually means in practice. Most people said they would like clarification – but the situation is often intrinsically complex and hard to define. Because they don't understand what happens within and between the organisations which hold their PI, participants were not themselves able to provide a comprehensive definition, but I have pieced together the following analysis from all the things people said:

a) Information is normally collected in connection with a particular transaction, which should define purpose, uses and access. It helps to visualise a box round the transaction.

b) In the normal course of events PI should stay within the original transaction box:

- only available to and used by those it was given to
- only used for the purposes implied by the transaction.

c) The nature and scope of the transaction box should be explained as clearly as possible to those who provide their PI – it will probably not follow organisational or geographical boundaries.

d) Disclosure of PI both within and outside that box should be parsimonious:

- only given to those who need to know
- only the information required for the job in hand.

e) Movement outside the original transaction box should be avoided where possible – and where it is found necessary it should be:

- limited in scale
- controlled through appropriate procedures or gateways
- notified to subjects (unless already obvious)
- cleared with subjects where the information or pathways may be sensitive.

I conclude that a transaction-based concept of confidentiality is useful because it allows data to follow pathways which are efficient for the customer without opening licence for wider disclosure.

Recommendation 1: The Department should consider developing a transaction-based model as a basis for structuring, controlling and explaining use of PI. This matches the way the public thinks about the subject, and would allow limited and controlled inter-organisational sharing – eg for Housing Benefit and Unemployment Benefit transactions.

4) Controlled flexibility: Many participants expressed a desire for confidentiality on the one hand, and for efficient service and minimisation of system abuse on the other. Some flexibility seems necessary – a balance has to be struck. Most participants want exceptions to be made where there is an important need to do so – for example they don't want confidentiality to damage children at risk, prevent proper response to emergencies, or protect serious criminals. But they would like such exceptions to be:

- kept to a reasonable minimum; and
- controlled and accountable.

They do not want confidentiality simply to be sacrificed in the name of 'efficiency'.

5) Different types of information: The degree of participant concern about confidentiality seemed to depend on two kinds of factor:

- partly on the *context* – things you would happily tell your doctor you wouldn't say to your bank manager, and vice versa
- partly on the *nature of the information* concerned – topics like finance and health were often thought specially sensitive (although even objectively trivial information can also arouse privacy concerns, particularly in large quantity).

Recommendation 2: DSS should consider classifying the sensitivity of different kinds of PI, and grading restrictions on access and use accordingly.

6) Reliability: People often expressed lively worries about reliability matters – including problems with:

- wrong, outdated, incomplete, misleading or opinion-based information
- data security – unauthorised access or disclosure (including leakage through staff turnover, staff disaffection or corruption).

7) Safeguards and controls: Participants would like to feel that there are safeguards and controls about the use of PI – but are not sure how far this is the case. Knowledge of the Data Protection Act seems patchy (and usually poor), and again people don't usually know what internal policies or procedures organisations have. Some suggested that:

- staff should be classified for access to PI
- levels of information should be similarly classified
- disclosures should be controlled through various kinds of authorisation or gateway, or limited as far as possible to confirming key points rather than making en bloc transfers of data.

Many people feel they have a moral right to know and to correct the PI organisations hold about them, but legal subject access rights are usually very poorly known – especially in relation to government departments. There also seem to be many doubts about being able to exercise such rights effectively.

Recommendation 3: Since the public are concerned about the accuracy of PI the Department should review (and where necessary strengthen) procedures for:

- checking and updating the accuracy and validity of PI

- safeguarding and controlling access and use
- training managers and staff in data security and confidentiality, to ensure high and consistent standards
- enabling effective public access (see below).

8) Sharing and pooling PI: Organisations can have a spectrum of possible information relationships, ranging from completely pooled data through different levels of request and authorisation to a complete refusal to share. The public do not know what the present situation is, but most would like to see different kinds of relationship, depending on the kind of organisation, the kind of information, and the purpose for which it is used.

Participants felt that sharing of information between bodies has many *disadvantages* for the subject, including:

- wider access and use (harder to control or even know about)
- loss of privacy
- proliferation of any errors
- greater risks of leaks or misuse
- transfer of power from individuals to organisations, and so on.

Some also mentioned possible *advantages*, but these tend to be less obvious (and sometimes less credible):

- better *for individuals* – information is available where and when needed, services may be delivered quicker, form-filling might be kept down, and help might be got more effectively to those in need
- and better *for the system* – more efficient working, better chance of cutting down fraud and crime.

Most participants seemed happy for information to pass between bodies who are legitimately connected to a particular transaction (like the Benefits Agency and a Housing Benefit authority) – *providing* it is directly relevant to that transaction, only disclosed to relevant and authorised staff, and explained in advance. This kind of sharing is likely to be efficient for both the agencies and their customers.

However, mass transfer or pooling of data was not generally approved by participants, particularly with bodies which are not party to the original transaction. The general view seems to be that:

- there should be a serious and valid reason for wanting to share information about an individual outside the transaction box – important enough to over-ride confidentiality

- there should be suitable procedures for authorising the transfer (more or less stringent depending on the particular context)
- only data relevant to the purpose should be disclosed
- as far as possible the subjects should be informed, if not consulted.

9) DSS: DSS is a very familiar body, but the details of its structure and functions were often vague to participants. The agency-based restructuring is not well known even to many claimants, and 'DHSS' is still the most common term. DSS still sometimes has a poor image, particularly among inner-city dwellers, young people and benefit claimants. This sometimes made participants wary and mistrustful about the way it uses information.

DSS by its nature collects and holds many of the kinds of information which participants regard as most private and sensitive – details of income, savings, and sometimes health, paternity, cohabitation etc. While conceding that this is to some extent inevitable, some feel the Department collects more (and more intrusive) PI than it ought to. Requirements to provide information about partners or other adult family members can be particularly sensitive. Lack of privacy in local office interviews is also sometimes a grievance.

Recommendation 4: Because of concerns about the amount of very 'private' information the Department asks for it should:

- ensure that it does not collect more PI than is strictly needed
- clarify the reasons for collecting sensitive information – as far as practicable, given the conflicting need to avoid increasing length or density of claim forms
- consider enabling partners to make separate returns where necessary
- improve privacy in offices where PI is given by the public.

DSS is not thought to explain what happens to the information collected. My brief inspection of some forms and leaflets suggests that practice is very variable, and that matters are never really explained in the terms people want. Satisfactory clarification would be difficult to achieve – but not in my view impossible.

Clarification of policy and practice would not only help customers by dispelling some of the current uncertainty, but may also have public relations value for the Department, which is at present widely suspected of handling PI less responsibly than its current policies imply. There may well be credibility problems in getting the message across.

Recommendation 5: The public would like to know more about what happens to the information the Department collects, which should be clarified. From my general experience this probably needs:

- brief statements on forms and leaflets – but clearer, more explicit, more prominent and better harmonised than at present
- a fuller set of published guidelines, made available:
  - for both public and internal use
  - in a brief leaflet and in more extended form.

Clarification should be as specific and concrete as possible – unexplained and generalised references to 'confidentiality' or to statutes do not aid understanding. The following points need clarifying – ideally using a transaction-based model (see above):

- the purposes for which PI is collected and used, and the limits to these purposes
- who has access to PI (within and outside the Department)
- under what circumstances it can be disclosed to outside bodies or individuals (and to whom)
- how access and use is safeguarded and controlled
- how long PI is kept, and how often updated
- how people can check their own records (see below).

Most people I talked to think they should be able to see their DSS records – but are not at all sure:

- whether they are legally entitled to do so
- how they could go about it
- whether they would get the truth
- and, sometimes, whether asking might count against them in some way.

Recommendation 6: In view of public confusion about subject access rights the Department should:

- publicise to customers the fact that they have a legal entitlement to see, verify and where necessary correct their PI
- publicise any limitations to this entitlement
- clarify how people should go about it if they want to inspect their records
- make it clear that they have a moral as well as a legal access right, and that exercising it will in no way penalise them or damage their interests
- ensure that suitable systems are in place, and that this service is delivered effectively, and in a willing and friendly way.

The Department might also consider developing a more interactive synthesis of data collection and subject access. IT makes it practicable to give people print-outs of information already held to correct, complete or endorse when they make a new claim. This should be more effective than a purely passive subject access right, and could also reduce the amount of (very unpopular) form-filling.

10) Disclosure to other bodies: Response to a series of detailed disclosure scenarios was interesting. It suggests that most people think:

- there should be an overarching commitment to confidentiality, only set aside for compelling reasons
- situations like children at risk are important enough to over-ride confidentiality, but such cases often involve wider issues concerning the best interests of the child, which (as some people pointed out) a Department like DSS may not be best placed to resolve, and which may be the proper territory of other agencies
- 'serious' crime is also thought important enough to over-ride confidentiality (in the scenarios I presented drug dealing rather than shop-lifting was seen in this light) – but disclosure to the police is seen as a significant action which should normally require reasonably high level authority
- helping 'good causes' does not justify breaching confidentiality
- DSS should never release information to commercial companies or for commercial purposes
- conversely, private sector organisations should not provide PI to DSS, except with court orders in the case of serious crime or fraud
- DSS should not provide addresses of debtors except after due process, and then only to the police or courts
- DSS should not provide PI to employers and landlords – except routine administrative details in the former case
- verification is preferable to outright disclosure of PI
- views about cross-checking government databases vary and are often ambivalent – but any checks should be selective and justified by reasonable suspicion
- it is all right to release anonymised information for purely statistical purposes.

Most participants agreed that information directly relating to specific transactions should be shared between DSS and other bodies – notably the Employment Service for UB and local authorities for HB. Such sharing is seen to benefit everyone – but they still want it limited, controlled, and clearly explained to claimants.

Most people feel that general sharing of PI between government departments should not be increased. Sharing should again be selective, controlled and justified – and kept to a reasonable minimum. Many oppose block transfers of information, and the idea of a centralised government PI database is usually felt to smack too much of Big Brother.

Other than for Housing Benefit purposes, people did not usually favour exchanges between DSS and LAs. DSS data should only go to social workers with their client's consent, or in exceptional cases of risk or need – and then with suitable controls.

Information might need to be shared with the police in emergencies or cases of serious crime – but people wanted fairly high-level authorisation procedures, justified only by exceptional circumstances.

Almost all participants wanted firm bi-directional firewalls between DSS and private sector organisations, only breachable through court orders.

Most felt that DSS should not exchange information with the voluntary sector – excepting advice agencies with explicit client consent.

Recommendation 7: In the light of public concern about where and when PI might leave the Department, DSS should affirm its over-riding commitment to confidentiality, and clarify:

- the kinds of situation in which this might be set aside
- its information relationships with different kinds of body in the public and private sectors.

Information flows could usefully be opened up along the lines of specific transactional relations (eg UB and HB) where necessary to improve service delivery – but where this happens it should be made clear to customers.

11) Internal disclosure: Most people seem fairly happy that information can be transferred between DSS agencies (since the Department is still largely seen as one organisation engaged in related functions) – although some have misgivings about including the CSA. However many people's preference would still be for some internal controls and gateways to ensure:

- that only relevant information is transferred
- that access is confined to relevant and authorised staff
- that highly sensitive information is particularly carefully safeguarded.

Recommendation 8: The Department should:

- review its rules and procedures for controlling internal access to PI
- consider a system of access coding for staff, ideally related to a classification of information sensitivity (see above).

12) DSS policies: The current policies and practices of DSS as expressed in the scenarios mostly commanded very widespread support among participants – although these were not always believed to represent practice on the ground.

Recommendation 9: The Department should broadly maintain the policies expressed in the scenarios, since these seem widely approved. There seems no case for radical change.

However, in the light of public scepticism the Department should take any necessary steps to make sure that these widely endorsed policies are in practice consistently implemented on the ground, and are made clear to the public.

13) Likely effects of policy change: It is difficult to assess how changes of confidentiality policy would affect people, since many are unaware of the current policy, and probably tend to exaggerate the amount of disclosure. People often suggest that reducing confidentiality would make the public:

- more reluctant to supply information
- more likely to falsify
- less likely to claim.

These effects do seem likely, but it is impossible from current evidence to guess their magnitude. Some pointed out that information is largely given under compulsion, and that not claiming is simply not an option for people with no other means. It may well be that take-up would nevertheless sometimes fall – but it would take larger-scale research to identify likely cases.

Loss of confidentiality would be seen by many as destroying one side of an implied bargain – people provide information they would rather keep to themselves, and the authorities reciprocally agree to keep this confidential. If authorities break the bargain this removes the moral obligation on individuals to comply fully and honestly with what is asked.

An overt retreat from confidentiality seems likely to damage public trust – and given the prevailing fragility of this trust it seems more useful to try mending fences through sensible strengthening, affirmation and clarification of confidentiality rather than to risk weakening it. Again, however, it is difficult to predict the practical outcome of either course on actual behaviour.

14) Overall conclusion: The confidentiality of personal information is a complex issue. Members of the public generally seem unclear about what happens at present, but there is a good deal of latent disquiet about the subject. Most people have conflicting desires:

- on the one hand they want it to be available enough for the efficient conduct of their own affairs, and they do not want confidentiality to act as a shield for serious wrong-doing

- but on the other hand they also want confidentiality to be treated as a serious issue, protected by effective controls and not lightly set aside.

Most people were not aware of the Department's current policies in relation to confidentiality and the disclosure of PI, but they tended to approve these policies as they were explained to them through the disclosure scenarios. The general feeling was that these policies should be broadly maintained, but clarified and better explained to the public.

Recommendation 10: In the light of the foregoing analysis the Department should not weaken its current commitment to confidentiality, which would not only go against the drift of public opinion, but might also possibly risk:

- increasing public unwillingness to give full, frank and honest information
- reducing take-up in some quarters
- further weakening of public trust.

2 THE STUDY

2.1 Objective

The Department of Social Security is reviewing its policy on confidentiality relating to information about its customers. The Department's current policy is that information provided by customers is held and used only for the purpose for which it is supplied – eg assessing entitlement and paying benefits. The only exceptions are those covered by statute – eg passing information to local authorities for Housing Benefit purposes.

The policy review arises not from any intention on the Department's part to change policy, but from:

- progressive change in the general information environment, and
- increasing pressures for information exchange from other branches of government.

The purpose of the current study is to provide input from the public, which is vital to any policy review. It is designed to yield information about relevant public perceptions, attitudes and behaviour – specifically:

a) what people believe or assume happens at present

b) what they think *should* happen

c) how this impacts on the way they behave – and particularly whether different approaches to confidentiality might affect propensity to claim or not to claim.

2.2 General method

The study is based mainly on qualitative research methods, using both group discussions and individual depth interviews.

Qualitative fieldwork was preceded by a review of available literature, designed to establish what information already exists, and provide input to the main study (Chapter 3).

2.3 Qualitative study

The uses organisations make of personal information is a highly complex subject, about which many people have strong feelings, but only a limited repertoire of ready-made ideas (see 4.1).

The research is based on qualitative group discussion methods, small in scale and not intended to provide statistical evidence. Unstructured qualitative research methods were chosen because they yield a broad understanding of the way people think and feel, and can help participants to work through the subject and explore their feelings in a considered way.

The report presents this understanding, which draws not only on the specific comments made by participants (which are widely quoted, both verbatim and indirectly) but also on the whole tone and pattern of the discussion.

The qualitative study is based on 16 interview sessions involving 69 people from 68 households[1]:

- 8 group discussions (averaging 7.5 people per group)
- 8 individual depth interviews (including one couple).

2.3.1 Sample

The sample was selected by quota sampling methods. It drew from the whole adult population (16+) – but rather than simply taking a straight cross section each session was focused on a particular segment, defined by several key variables – for example education level, receipt of benefits or age.

The study included people in work as well as benefit recipients and retired people, because we wanted to sound the views of the whole population. However the number of benefit recipients was deliberately upweighted, since they would have a wider range of experience to draw on in discussing the ways DSS uses personal information. The sample split about 60:40 between benefit recipients and non-recipients ('benefits' being defined for this purpose as Income Support, Unemployment Benefit, Family Credit, Housing Benefit and a range of sickness or disability benefits).

2.3.2 Further details of method

Further details of method and sample are in Annex I, a sample profile in Annex II, and the recruitment questionnaire in Annex III.

2.3.3 Areas

The work was carried out in four areas (England only):

- London (Islington)
- South not London (Reading)
- Midlands (Birmingham Northfields)
- North (Huddersfield).

2.3.4 Stimulus material

It was anticipated that people's repertoire of ideas about the topic would be limited – they might not have developed views, and would need help in unpacking their thoughts on such a complex and amorphous problem.

A range of non-directive stimulus material was therefore devised to help focus thinking about certain aspects of the topic. This was mainly used in the second half of the conversation, once people's spontaneous perceptions had been well ventilated. It was deployed selectively – not all of it was

---

1 A couple took part in one of the depth interviews.

used in every session, and its use depended on the progress of each interview, and on the time available.

The materials comprised:

- 40 specific scenarios detailing possible disclosure situations (4.3.4 and Annex V)
- a schematic diagram of various bodies who might exchange information (4.3.5)
- lists of:
  - different types of information (4.2.6)
  - different types of relationship between givers and receivers of information (4.2.1).

2.3.5 The group sessions The discussions were informal and conversational. They worked from a loose topic guide (Annex IV), not a set questionnaire. All were tape-recorded in stereo, and the tapes transcribed for detailed analysis. Participants were paid £15 a head to cover any expenses in attending sessions, and as an incentive to turn out.

2.3.6 Responsibilities The project was designed and carried out by Alan Hedges, who conducted all the interviews, analysed the responses and reported the findings. Stimulus material was designed jointly by Alan Hedges and DSS – the Department mainly devised the scenarios, and the researcher originated the remainder. Recruitment of participants was by Plus Four Market Research.

2.3.7 Limitations and caveats The sample is small and geographically limited. Qualitative research of this kind is designed to yield understanding rather than statistical evidence. Numbers are not usually quoted – and where they are, they must not be taken as reliable statistical statements about the national population.

2.3.8 Timing Fieldwork was carried out in two halves, with interim feedback:

- **November and early December 1995:** literature review, first half of fieldwork (London and Reading), and interim debrief
- **Mid-January to end February 1996:** second half of fieldwork (Midlands and North), final debrief and report.

2.3.9 Verbatims Considerable use is made of verbatim quotations, because these give an important flavour of the way people think, talk and feel. However they are included only for illustration, and **should always be read in the context of the surrounding commentary**. Presence or absence of quotes does not denote importance, since some important points are hard to illustrate in this way.

Verbatims are preceded by the letters 'M' or 'F' showing the sex of the speaker. Remarks preceded by 'I' are from the interviewer. Each comment or piece of dialogue is followed by a label in brackets showing:

1. the area ('Lon' = London, 'Sth' = South, 'Mid' = Midlands, 'Nth' = North).
2. the type of people in the session, where relevant: for example 'lone parent', 'benefits' (benefit recipients, as defined), 'low-TEA' (people who left school at the minimum age), 'mid-TEA' (people leaving after A level), 'graduates' (educated to degree level or equivalent).
3. the age group, where relevant.

Discussions were carefully transcribed, but errors can occur in verbatims (particularly in specialised terminology or local names). I apologise for any such.

2.3.10 *This report*

The report is organised into 4 chapters, plus 7 annexes:

Chapter 1: Overview summarising key conclusions and recommendations
Chapter 2: The study
Chapter 3: Literature review
Chapter 4: Study findings
- 4.1 Personal information and confidentiality
- 4.2 Using and disclosing PI
- 4.3 DSS and its use of PI

Annexes I to VII contain:

I Methods and sample
II Sample profile
III Recruitment questionnaire
IV Topic guide
V Stimulus material
VI List of sources consulted
VII Letter of authority

2.3.11 *Terms used*

Terms and abbreviations used in this report include:

- CSA Child Support Agency
- DPA Data Protection Act
- DPR Data Protection Registrar
- FC Family Credit
- HB Housing Benefit
- IS Income Support
- IR Inland Revenue
- IT Information technology
- LA Local Authority
- NI National Insurance

- PI Personal information
- UB Unemployment Benefit

3 LITERATURE REVIEW

A brief literature review preceded the main study. The main material reviewed is listed at Annex VI. The main conclusions of the review are as follows.

There is a good deal of material which relates to the whole field of personal information, confidentiality, privacy and data protection. However, there is little direct research evidence about public perceptions, and very little recent data indeed. Most of the material relates to:

- the information technology (IT) aspects of confidentiality – computer technology, security of systems, etc
- the legal aspects – analysis of the legal situation (often relating to data protection law, and sometimes including international comparisons)
- policy analysis – including international comparisons of policy and legislation
- confidentiality of information collected for research purposes
- review of issues and practice in particular sectors – usually healthcare and social services.

Texts on these subjects sometimes contain some relevant material, but only the more promising material has been examined extensively for this review.

Material from the review is quoted in various parts of Chapter 4. The texts worth commenting on here are as follows.

The Data Protection Registrar has commissioned a limited amount of market research. Three items are worth mention:

- The Appendix of his 10th Annual Report (June 1994) contains summaries of some annual omnibus surveys, mainly covering levels of awareness and concern. This is quoted at relevant points in Chapter 4 below. It tends to show fairly high levels of concern about PI and fairly low levels of awareness of the Data Protection Act (DPA) (see 4.2.4.1).
- Qualitative research by Alan Hedges (1986) covered general public attitudes to privacy, confidentiality and data protection. The findings provide useful general background, and seem broadly congruent with the present study.
- A rather limited qualitative study of personal information as used by DSS and DVLC (One World Research & Communications, 1993). The

DSS element was based only on 3 group discussions among Income Support claimants. The study suggested that worries about data abuse mainly revolve round private companies (notably junk mail lists and credit rating agencies). People were hostile to the idea of government departments providing information to commercial companies, but reactions varied about the idea of exchanging information between departments. Use of PI was a less salient preoccupation for benefit customers than getting their benefits and being properly treated – there was a lot of negative imagery about DSS. There were complaints about collection of excessive and irrelevant PI, and about lack of privacy in offices. People were generally more worried about their neighbours knowing their business than DSS staff.

Apart from these I was not able to find directly relevant survey evidence, except:

- quotations from research done from the Younger Committee – quite interesting but rather out of date (1972)
- abstracts from a few American studies, which may or may not apply to the UK.

A quantity of books, papers and abstracts was considered. The main items are listed in Annex E. The following books are worth mentioning for general background interest, but only parts of these texts are directly relevant:

Regulating Privacy, Colin J Bennett (1992)
Personal Information, Privacy and the Law, Raymond Wacks (1989)
Privacy and Human Rights, James Michael (1994).

4 FINDINGS OF THE STUDY

4.1 Personal information and confidentiality

This section looks at:

- general attitudes to personal information (PI) and confidentiality
- the levels of concern about the subject.

4.1.1 What is personal information (PI)?

The term 'personal information' has two related but distinct popular meanings:

- At its broadest it simply means *any information about identifiable individuals* – in this sense 'personal' just means 'pertaining to a person'.
- More narrowly it also means information about those people which is *highly 'private' or 'sensitive'* – for example people use it in this sense when they complain about being asked 'personal' questions.

These two concepts are not sharply separated in many minds, and can cause confusion – people sometimes drift from one meaning to the other.

4.1.2 Ownership of information

Most people feel that personal information about them belongs to them, not to the body that happens to hold it. Passing it over on a form or in answer to questions does not make it the property of the collecting organisation.

> *M: 'You've lent them your information and they should treat it with respect, and not just chuck it around and bandy it around'*
>
> (Sth, benefits, 30–44)

In general this seems to apply to information about individuals which is created by the organisation as well as information provided by the person. Thus the contributions record or record of benefits received still seems to 'belong' to the person concerned, even though it was produced by DSS agencies and not by the individual it relates to. The same principles would usually be seen to apply to its storage and use.

A few people argued that National Insurance numbers are provided by the State and are therefore the State's property – but most people again seem to see these as belonging in the domain of the individual.

4.1.3 Level of awareness and concern

Concern about issues relating to personal information seems very widespread. Most people seem generally uneasy about the way information about them is circulated and used. Only a few participants were completely unconcerned about it.

F: 'I'm quite a private person, for no particular reason, and I'm quite worried that people know so much about my life and my lifestyle'
I: 'What sort of people?'
F: 'I'm talking about like the DHSS, the marketing business, all this rubbish coming through your door, people wanting you to spend money with them and knowing your date of birth, how old you are – I like to tell people things rather than people find out'

(Mid, graduates, 35–44)

A quantitative framework for the levels of concern is provided by several omnibus survey questions from Annex 5 of the 10th Annual report of the Data Protection Registrar (DPR). Annual survey results are quoted for the years 1992, '93 and '94, each year based on a sample of about 1000 adults.

Members of the public were asked to choose from a list of issues those they considered very important.

	1992 %	1993 %	1994 %
Proportion saying the following are very important			
Preventing crime on the streets	91	85	86
Improving standards of education	82	78	79
Unemployment	80	78	73
Protecting people's rights to personal privacy	78	66	66
Protecting freedom of speech	67	53	57
Inflation	66	46	53
Making sure women have equal rights	61	57	53
Protecting the rights of minority groups	40	40	36

I have sorted DPR's table into descending order on 1994 values. Privacy is not so big an issue as crime prevention, education or unemployment – but bigger than freedom of speech, inflation, women's rights or minority rights. The 'privacy' percentage was higher in 92 than in the two later years – but so were most of the figures quoted, and there is no sign of a continuing trend.

This question talks generally about 'privacy', which is a wider subject than just protecting personal information. DPR's next table looks at different kinds of privacy concern.

Members of the public were asked to name the five privacy issues which were of most concern to them. They were given a list of 9 issues to choose from.

Proportion saying the following are of most concern:	1992 %	1993 %	1994 %
Protecting the privacy of your own home/property	78	79	75
Keeping personal information/details private	76	73	71
Being able to do what I want in my own home	64	66	62
People telling me what to do/interfering with my life	58	58	56
Maintaining freedom of movement/speech/religion	50	53	56
Organisations building up files of information about me	52	49	53
Individuals prying into my business	52	53	53
Stopping unwanted mail/telephone calls/selling	51	49	47

Again I have sorted DPR's table into descending order on 1994 values. Among the eight aspects of privacy listed, 'keeping personal information/details private' ranks second in the percentage choosing it as of most concern. Both were mentioned by about three-quarters of the sample. 'Organisations building up files of information about me' ranks lower, but still with 53% mention.

Interestingly, although junk-mail/junk calls were mentioned spontaneously in my research more often than almost any other issue, they figure last in this table.

Members of the public were asked to say how concerned they were about the amount of information kept about them by various organisations.

	1992 %	1993 %	1994 %
Very concerned	39	33	36
Quite concerned	34	35	36
Neither/nor	8	11	9
Not very concerned	12	15	13
Not at all concerned	5	5	5

In 1994, 72% of DPR's sample were 'very concerned' or 'quite concerned' about the amount of information organisations keep about them, compared with only 18% who were 'not very concerned' or 'not at all concerned'. 36% were at the top of the scale against only 5% at the bottom. This confirms that there is widespread concern.

Colin Bennett (*Regulating privacy*, p37-40) quotes a few survey figures[2].

2 These are only of broad background relevance, and I have not studied the original sources.

- The British Younger Committee's 1972 survey showed that privacy invasion[3] was considered the most important of social or civil rights issues – although ranked lower than economic matters like unemployment and inflation. 38% thought it 'quite important', 29% 'very important', and 16% 'extremely important'. 58% thought people had less privacy than they used to have.

- In Gallup's "Six Nation Survey on Orwell's '1984'" the statement 'There is no real privacy because the government can learn anything it wants about you' was apparently endorsed by 59% of Britons (and 68% of Canadians, 47% of Americans, but only 18% of Germans).

- Harris polls in the United States showed that the percentages thinking that 'the present uses of computers are an actual threat to personal privacy in this country' rose from 38% in 1974 through 41% in '77 to 51% in '83. The '83 poll apparently showed that 'a significant majority of American citizens believed that personal files were kept without their knowledge, that they did not trust either private or public organisations to use that information fairly and properly, and that new federal laws were needed to provide adequate safeguards.'

However, my research suggests that people's worries are usually somewhat unfocused, and often not mapped out in detail. Indeed most participants did not seem to have given much organised thought to the subject before. They just feel patches of vague unease, sometimes with occasional outcrops of more specific worries.

> *F: 'Like it is a bit eerie that they know so much. The more you think about it the more like eerie it does get, how much they know'*
>
> (Mid, lone parent, 30–44)

> *I: 'Do you ever think about what happens to the information you provide?'*
> *F: 'Occasionally, and it worries me when I do. Well when you suddenly try and begin to piece together the different pieces of information you've given to people who you then realise will be in contact with each other – you realise that a picture of yourself is being built up in departments that you have no control over, and that you can't know in what way it's going to be mistreated or used against you in some way which – well I suppose I've heard enough horror stories of people having found that their names are on some sort of blacklist, or information has been passed between other departments without them having even known it was passed, and a decision's been taken by this department on the grounds of something else without them having known that information was being used against them, and having no chance to defend themselves against some kind of wrong accusation'*

---

3 Not specifically from personal information.

M: 'It's only the fact you've focused our minds on this this afternoon that I'm giving it any thought, otherwise I wouldn't have given it any thought whatsoever'

(Lon, benefits, 16–39)

This situation of widespread but unfocused concern arises mainly from the combination of two factors:

- On the one hand many people believe that personal information now circulates more widely and freely than it used to (or than it should do), and this is the main source of concern.
- On the other hand there is also a sense of ignorance about what actually does happen – what is known about you by whom, where the information comes from, how it is handled, why they have it, what happens to it, or where it might go to next. This is why the concerns seem unfocused – people are often vaguely unhappy with what seems to be happening, but since they don't really *know,* their anxieties remain diffuse and shadowy. However, the uncertainty is itself often disturbing – the fact that they don't know what goes on is in itself a source of concern.

M: 'I think it's very important'
M: 'Yes I'd like to know where all the information goes'
F: 'Yes when technology's sort of spreading'
F: 'Yes I'm very surprised at stuff that comes through my door that I know nothing about and I wonder where people have (a) got my name and address from, and, (b) how they knew like for example that my house insurance was up on a certain month when it's a company I've never used. I find it quite daunting that somebody might know that amount of personal information about me, and I don't know where it's come from'

(Mid, graduates, 35–44)

M: 'They don't say, "Can we access this information, sign here", therefore we don't know. How am I supposed to give an opinion when I've got no information'
M: 'I'm 44 years old and I do not know what is happening to this information, and I think that I should know – and it's something I haven't thought about up until now'

(Lon, benefits, 16–44)

M: 'When you say you've got no privacy, you don't know whether you have or not, that's the thing that gets me. None of us know what they actually know about us'

(Mid, benefits, 45–64)

Their impression that personal information now circulates more freely comes from several sources:

a) an image of the developing power of information technology (IT), which seems to facilitate the movement of information (see 4.1.8)

b) periodic incidents in their own lives which leave them puzzled about 'where they got my name from', or 'how they know so much about me' (see 4.1.3.1)

c) a sense of changing organisational cultures – organisations in the public as well as the private sector often seem to be getting less scrupulous and professional, and perhaps more aggressively commercial.

The level of concern often grew during the discussions as participants considered the subject in more depth. There seems to be a lot of latent unease which is brought to the surface by prolonged consideration of the subject.

Some people seem fatalistic and resigned about the uses of PI – they may not like their data so freely circulated, but they don't think there's anything they can do about it. This doesn't stop them feeling uneasy about it, but it tends to inhibit it from becoming a front-of-mind concern – why spend your time worrying about what you can't remedy?

I: 'On the whole do you trust government departments to make responsible use and take reasonable care of the personal information they have about you?'
F: 'Well you have to, you haven't any choice have you?'
M: 'Well you've just got to hope'
F: 'You've no guarantees have you?'

(Mid, low-TEA, 45–64)

F: 'Well I've become resigned to the fact that everywhere you go you're being followed by a video camera practically these days, so everybody knows everything about everyone. All around the country you've got computers with all your information stashed away for anybody to access. You can't fight it so I'm resigned to it'

(Lon, pensioners)

F: 'We're all sitting here saying what we should have, but we're not gonna get that, so like there's no point in saying it'

(Lon, benefits, 16–39)

A small minority are not concerned at all about the uses of PI. They usually seem to be people who have:

- a low need for personal privacy – they don't much mind who has information about them, or what they know
- a feeling that their affairs are in good order, and that they have 'nothing to hide'
- a reasonable degree of trust that the system will not seriously misuse information about them.

F: 'I've got no reason to worry because I live my life according to the laws and according to the rules'

(Lon, lone parent, 16–29)

Phrases like 'if you've got nothing to hide you've nothing to fear' were quite often heard, particularly early in the conversation – although such sentiments were quite often contested by others, and even those who said these things often went on to take the view that better controls and safeguards are needed, and that too much pooling of information is undesirable. The thrust of the research suggests that it would be simplistic and misleading to assume that only people with guilty secrets want confidentiality. Concerns are often more broadly based, and may include fear of errors or unauthorised disclosure, desire for privacy, concerns about centralisation of State power, and so on (see 4.1.7, 4.2.2, 4.2.3).

M: 'I've got nothing to hide, so there's nothing to worry about'
F: 'It isn't a question of having something to hide, it's a question of your personal information, and it should only be released if you want it to be, or you want to tell somebody about it'

(Mid, low-TEA, 45–64)

M: '"If you've got nothing to hide you've got nothing to fear" – that's the despot's phrase through the ages, that's a phrase that could have quite happily sat with Hitler's Germany'

(Mid, graduates, 35–44)

F: 'I don't believe this simple idea of being innocent and having nothing to fear anyway – there's still a loss of control about it, which is a kind of diminishment of your privacy and civil liberties'

(Lon, benefits, 16–39)

PI tends to be a background concern rather than a front-line worry. Practical issues like unemployment or housing are usually much more pressing.

4.1.3.1 Public and private sectors

PI concerns are usually more front-of-mind in relation to the private sector, because most people get frequent reminders of the way their names are used by commercial companies. The following seemed to be the main sources of participants' concern.

a) Targeted junk mail: Junk mail lands almost daily on most doormats. This is often found irritating for various reasons – and telephone sales calls are even more intrusive. However the main relevance of sales approaches to the present study is that people are often puzzled about 'where they got my name from' – particularly since direct mail is increasingly targeted to particular market segments, which seems to imply knowledge of the recipient beyond mere name and address. People know in a general way that mailing lists are passed on (and indeed 'sold') from one organisation to another – they don't know exactly how or how often this happens, but most assume the practice is very widespread[4]. Many find the thought of someone 'selling their name' disturbing and illegitimate – it seems like selling their personal property without them being asked or even informed[5].

> *F: 'I find all sorts of things coming through my door with my name and address on and I don't know where they've got it from'*
> *I: 'Does that disturb you?'*
> *F: 'Well yes it does, because it isn't something I've given permission about. Why has this come? How have they got my name?'*
>
> (Mid, low-TEA, 45–64)

> *M: 'At one time banks, they used to be confidential, but I don't know what they pass on. Many years ago I was made redundant, I had some money so I put it in the bank straightaway and in a fortnight I had a letter, "Apply for your American Express card". Now in all my life they had never bothered me with American Express. Now how did American Express know that I'd got something?'*
>
> (Mid, benefits, 45–64)

> *F: 'I know my house insurance is due or my contents insurance is due for renewal, but how come I've had in the last fortnight five letters from five completely different companies offering me deals when I've never dealt with those companies before. So how come my name, address and details have landed on their computer screens or whatever?'*
>
> (Mid, graduates, 35–44)

b) Postcoded retail information: Many also find it worrying that shops or suppliers seem to know a lot more about them than they would expect – and again this raises questions about where the information came from, and how the company got hold of it. Often the PI seems to be accessed through something like postcode. This seems mystifying, and sometimes gives rise to fears that such occurrences might be just the tip of some larger PI iceberg.

> *F: 'I've tried to get credit to say buy a cooker and they've keyed in my post code and told me every address I've ever had. And two addresses I lived in are women's hostels that supposedly are meant to be PO Box numbers'*
> *F: 'Yeah, well that's the kind of thing that makes you wonder'*
> *F: 'Well my friend works for BT and I used to just chat to him on the phone,*

---

4 While writing this report I received a direct mail leaflet about the 1996 'Lists and Data Sources' directory, which offers 'over 5,600 UK-owned Business and Consumer lists'.

5 Some referred to opt-out boxes on forms, but the general view seems to be that it should be an opt-in process – that consent to use your name should be sought explicitly rather than assumed unless you take steps to object.

he didn't have my address, and then one day he phoned me up and he tapped me into a computer and he told me where I lived'

(Lon, benefits, 16–39)

F: 'They even were able to tell me my name and the number of my house, which rather surprised me – never asked for me name, just my post code'
F: 'I think it's quite efficient, I do'
F: 'I found it spooky – how the hell do they know all that about me, I've never spoken to them before'
M: 'I find it infringement of your privacy'

(Mid, low-TEA, 45–64)

M: 'Same as your post code, I rung up Swansea about my driving licence, querying it, what's your post code? So I give 'em me post code, and I couldn't even introduce meself on the phone, they know everything. Well your name, your address, your age, your driving convictions, everything, it's all there at the touch of a button'

(Nth, benefits, 40+)

c) Credit-rating agency activities: Those who come into contact with the activities of credit rating agencies are often even more disturbed about the range and nature of the information these bodies have about them.

M: 'You go into a shop they can do a credit check on you, they can find out things about you you don't know – and it don't take long either'

(Nth, benefits, 40+)

However, although the private sector often comes more quickly to mind, some people see the **public sector** as ultimately more significant – mainly because government and other authorities can be very important and powerful in their lives.

M: 'I find much more worrying the information the State has, and access to that information, accountability of that information. And I think MI5 hold something like one million files on British Citizens, which is quite daunting really, as well as the DSS'

(Mid, graduates, 35–44)

Traditionally, government bodies have seemed likely to be fairly secure and responsible users of PI, but some people are no longer so sure how far they trust them to maintain confidentiality. There seems to be growing fear in many quarters that they may misuse or disclose information, or share it with other government bodies – or even with the private sector. Distinction between public and private seems to be blurring.

I: 'On the whole would you feel that you would trust a government department to keep the information secure in that way or not?'
M: 'Well no I wouldn't'

F: 'It's the individuals that work there – it doesn't matter what rules, it's if they carry them out'
F: 'And it's the sheer volume of information on thousands of people'

(Mid, graduates, 35–44)

M: 'I think the majority of the general public that come in contact with Government agencies have no idea of what goes on. I've got no idea what happens to the information – I'm sure the information is mistreated, I'm sure there are agencies that obtain information about us, but technically shouldn't be obtaining that information. But I don't think that government – I think they're so disorganised they cannot secure the system'
M: 'I think there is legislation and I think there are rules there, but there are always people that for the right money will breach the rules – I'm not talking about some guy working in the local DSS, I'm talking about somebody higher up who a company would go to and say, "Look, it would be to our advantage to have a list of everybody that's claiming certain types of benefit – if we give you x thousand pounds or whatever, can you supply that?". I'm sure this goes on'

(Lon, benefits, 16–39)

M: 'This is why I think this information is coming from government offices. It's got to do'
F: 'They're getting it from somewhere aren't they?'
M: 'They've got to get it from somewhere – and it's private information'

(Nth, benefits, 60+)

M: 'The government won't tell ya who they passed it out to, which department has got your documentation – well between your tax, your DHSS, medical, they won't tell you where it's been passed'

(Nth, benefits, 40+)

F: 'We talked about civil service ethos and how it's all going down the tubes, maybe that's what it is in the end, whereas it used to be that public service was an honour and all the rest of it, and were prepared to take a fairly low salary for high security and feeling you were doing something – that's gone'

(Sth, graduates, 35–44)

Many people assume that government departments already exchange and share information to a greater extent than they probably do.

4.1.3.2 Knowledge and understanding

Knowledge and understanding are typically very limited. The public feel they are not told what happens to their personal information – and some are not sure they believe what they are told. Many feel the situation should be clarified by data users.

F: 'I think they (DSS) should explain to people, because you do divulge your whole life to them almost – and I divulged it hoping it would go no further than them'

(Sth, benefits, 45–64)

M: 'You need to know what information can be transferred and at what level it could be transferred, whose authorisation is going to allow certain information to be transferred. Another thing I'd be very keen to know is if I'm giving information to the Inland Revenue and it's going on to a database, I'd want to know what other databases it goes on to'

(Mid, graduates, 35–44)

F: 'I think they should tell you what they do with it. You see they get all this information and all these forms that you fill in, but they never actually tell you where those forms go to and where they stay, and how long they keep them for'
M: 'You can be assured complete confidentiality but you can never be sure'
M: 'That's it, we don't know what happens to it, who's got information about us'
M: 'You're told it's all confidential but obviously that's as far as you go, they've got your information and you walk off, so how do we know who's got rights to it and who hasn't, who can get access to it and who can't – you're told it's confidential'
I: 'Should you know?'
M: 'I think we should know yes'
F: 'Yeah definitely'
M: 'I think all our information, we should know exactly what happens to it'
M: 'It's just like telling one of your mates a secret and saying, "You won't pass it on", "Oh no, no I won't do" – but invariably it does get passed on'

(Nth, benefits, 40+)

The situation is intrinsically both complex and shadowy because it involves:

a) an enormous volume and variety of types of personal information, collected by different bodies for different purposes

b) a bewilderingly large number of public and private bodies, whose structure, functions, operations and relationships are often not well understood

c) information handling processes which are mostly invisible to the average citizen (or customer), and which therefore leave them guessing (and often suspecting) what actually goes on

d) information technology which makes it increasingly possible to move and share large volumes of data, and allows what seem to be separate departments or organisations to be increasingly interconnected.

M: 'The trouble is that we have so many centres today, not just local centres, gathering information – like in all the big cities like Newcastle, London, Leeds – and all this information goes to these places and then it's channelled back again'
F: 'It seems to be floating about'
M: 'Well I don't agree with that, I think it should be localised'

(Nth, benefits, 60+)

Most people therefore have a very limited picture indeed of what actually happens when they hand over information – where it goes, how it is stored, who is allowed to see and use it, how long it is kept, whether it moves from place to place or from department to department. They hand in a form or send a letter – and the information effectively vanishes from their ken. Parts of it may reappear periodically during later transactions when officials refer to it or call it up on computer screens, and this can furnish small clues about the way it is kept and used – people sometimes base broader inferences (correct or incorrect) on these. But in general the subject is shrouded in fog – they simply do not know what goes on. This is why their concerns tend to be unfocused.

> *F: 'I would have said that they're all piled on top of one another and then the person who deals with the claims and whatever does 'em all at the same time. They'd have to go elsewhere to be filed. I know they pass it from one department to another before it finally gets finished with. But I would assume like they deal with it and then it gets passed to whoever else and then finally gets filed away in your – must be awfully big folders. But I suppose now it's all micro chips or computer discs it's all filed under'*
>
> (Mid, lone parent, 30–44)

> *M: 'I assume it goes to the appropriate body but then after that I'm totally in the dark as I'm sure most of us are. More than one person gets your information I'm absolutely sure of that. On just the junk mail you get, somebody puts your name forward somewhere along the chain'*
>
> (Lon, pensioners)

> *F: 'That's probably what we'd like to know, where it does go'*
> *F: 'Probably go onto a central computer somewhere so everybody can take their little bits off it'*
>
> (Nth, 16–34)

Nor do most people feel they are able to dispel the fog. Again the situation is too complex – too many bodies, too many types of information. Unless people have highly specific concerns about a given body and a given type of information they simply would not know where to start – and many of the concerns are general rather than particular. Moreover many are not confident that they would in practice be able to find out anything useful and reliable even if they wanted to (see 4.2.5). So very few ever set out to find out more about their PI – most just accept that this is a subterranean activity which is largely unknowable.

The situation is also seen to be getting increasingly complex as the power and deployment of information technology takes off (see 4.1.8.2). Many people are fairly hazy about the way computers operate, but it is widely assumed that they interconnect in complex and (again) invisible ways.

4.1.4 Trust in organisations

Concern about the uses of PI depends partly on how far the public trust the bodies who have and use it. This research suggests that levels of trust are often fairly low at present, whether in government departments, other public sector bodies or the private sector. Suspicion seems fairly common, and outright cynicism seems rife in some quarters.

> *M: 'Well they say they're not meant to do it, but what they say and what they do are two different things'*
>
> (Lon, benefits, 16–29)

> *F: 'Having worked on the population census and people saying, "I'm not filling in where I'm working, I'm not telling you how much I earn, it'll go wider"'*
>
> (Mid, graduates, 35–44)

I have no direct evidence whether people were ever more trusting, but there is a general sense that public trust in the good faith of organisations has declined and is declining. People seem less ready to assume that government departments will be scrupulously professional, and more likely to suspect they may now do things for commercial rather than exclusively public service reasons. The dividing line between public service and commerce seems to have become blurred and private sector organisations (commercial by nature) now often seem to market more aggressively.

> *F: 'They constantly encourage you to use bank accounts to receive – so then all these government departments have got access to your daily bank balance. I'm sure they haven't officially, but I think the potential is there'*
> *I: 'Would the DSS know what was in your bank?'*
> *M: 'Banks are not allowed to do that. The bank's not allowed to reveal information about your account except to Customs and Excise'*
> *F: 'Or the police'*
> *F: 'Or government'*
>
> (Lon, benefits, 16–39)

> *M: 'What I'm against is spreading it to places where – well I don't know whether it happens or not, but I can quite imagine it happening, going to private companies. This is what I'm against. I'm not saying it's a general practice, but I think certain individuals are capable of it. Money talks'*
>
> (Nth, benefits, 60+)

> *M: 'I think they've mixed the commercial side of life in this country with the official side, and I think information's swapped very very easily'*
>
> (Mid, low-TEA, 45–64)

This lack of trust means that people are often suspicious and pessimistic about the ways in which PI is handled and used – processes which again they don't feel they can see or control.

The sample is too small for confident sub-group analysis (and the patterns were not entirely clear-cut), but mistrust seemed particularly common among:

- people in inner-city areas
- benefit claimants
- younger people[6].

The Data Protection Registrar's annual omnibus survey (*op cit*) asked members of the public to say how satisfied they were that various organisations can be trusted to keep and use information in a responsible way.

		1992 %	1993 %	1994 %
Doctors and the NHS	Satisfied	92	92	88
	Not satisfied	5	3	5
Banks and building societies	Satisfied	78	75	74
	Not satisfied	13	16	18
Police	Satisfied	72	78	72
	Not satisfied	15	12	16
Employers	Satisfied	74	72	69
	Not satisfied	11	11	13
Inland Revenue	Satisfied	68	68	67
	Not satisfied	17	15	18
Schools and colleges	Satisfied	66	70	63
	Not satisfied	12	7	10
DHSS	Satisfied	63	65	61
	Not satisfied	16	15	20
Shops and stores	Satisfied	36	32	35
	Not satisfied	41	40	36
Credit reference agencies	Satisfied	25	30	29
	Not satisfied	49	41	45
Mail order companies	Satisfied	23	23	22
	Not satisfied	57	54	51

6 Young people are quite interesting. On the one hand their personal affairs have not usually yet acquired much depth, so that there is less to know about them than there will be when they have their own homes, children, mortgages and so on. On the other hand they tend to be more sceptical about authority. Although anyone aged 16+ was eligible, in practice there were not many people in the sample aged under 20.

This table paints a rosier picture of trust than I found in my discussions[7], although the rank order is similar. I have resorted the table into descending order of 'satisfied' on '94 data. 'Doctors and the NHS' easily top the list with 88% satisfaction[8]. 'Banks and building societies' also do well with 74%. DSS comes 7th out of the 10 organisations – although still with a roughly 3:1 ratio between satisfied and not satisfied. In the latest survey about 1 in 5 were 'not satisfied' that DSS can be trusted. Commercial organisations (apart from banks and building societies) occupy the bottom three slots.

4.1.5 Attitudes to confidentiality

Most people instinctively feel they are entitled to confidentiality in the way their PI is handled – but many are not at all sure how far they get the confidentiality they think they deserve (and often suspect they do not). Many assume PI is more freely bandied about:

- than they would like, or feel is justified
- than is sometimes actually the case – some fears may be exaggerated through ignorance of what actually happens (although others also seem understated).

For many people it almost seems as if there is some kind of invisible underground network which trades in personal information. All they know is that information about them (and other individuals) seems to bob up in surprising places and in unaccountable ways. It seems there must by implication be channels and links they don't know about. 'Where did they get my name?' is a very pervasive question, often carrying a mixture of surprise, indignation and apprehension. As we saw in 4.1.3, many know that names and addresses get 'sold on' from one organisation to another for commercial purposes, and are disconcerted when shops and commercial organisations seem to know a surprising amount about them. It is experiences (and/or suspicions) like these which tend to suggest that confidentiality is not something they can take for granted, and that PI circulates more widely than they would like.

This makes some people worry about supplying information to commercial companies.

F: 'We bought a computer today at Dixon's on interest-free credit, so we had to fill in a form as long as your arm saying, "Do you own your house?", and all

---

7 This could reflect the differences between instant reactions in the quantitative survey, and thoughts that have been unpacked more in the present qualitative study. I have also often noted that questions about 'satisfaction' tend to produce bland and over-favourable results.

8 My evidence suggests that 'Doctors' would get a higher rating than 'the NHS'.

the other things – and the trouble is if you say, "I'm not going to tell you", they say, "Fine, well you don't have the interest-free credit". I mean you haven't got much choice'
M: 'That gets passed on'
F: 'Well I'm sure it probably does'
I: 'Would it ever actually make you decide that you weren't going to buy something or ask for credit because you were being asked those questions?'

M: 'I have in the past refused to rent a television because they asked too many questions'

(Sth, mid-TEA, 45–64)

F: 'Every time you go into a supermarket now they ask you to sign your name and address and join some kind of scheme, and give all sorts of information about where you live and what you normally buy'
F: 'Safeways has got an ABC card, it tells me how much I've shopped, how much I've spent, how many points I've got, and then I thought they literally know everything, I had to give my name and address to get that – they know how many items I bought in a year – Safeways can find that out'

(Lon, benefits, 16–39)

4.1.6 What does 'confidential' mean?

In principle the term 'confidential' seems to pose no problems – it has an obvious, commonsense and well-understood meaning, something along the following lines: If I give you information in confidence you are not to pass it on to someone else unless with my consent, or in ways which were mutually understood when I gave it to you.

F: 'I think if you fill a form in confidentially, then that should be what it is. If you go to a solicitor or a doctor you don't expect them to discuss you with Mrs. Jones up the road'

(Sth, mid-TEA, 45–64)

If personal information is given to someone as an individual then the confidence would normally be violated if they passed it on to anyone else. But people do not literally expect that information given to someone in an organisation will not be divulged to anyone else within the organisation. Sometimes it *must* be passed on in order to carry out the transaction in connection with which it was given. Imagine someone taking a car to a garage for servicing[9]. They provide PI both relating to themselves and to the car, but would not expect (or want) all this information to stay exclusively within service reception – the garage does not need to ask their permission before telling the mechanics who are to do the repairs what the problem is. They would also be free to pass (say) credit card details to the accounts department for billing purposes. This is

9 This example was not specifically suggested by participants, but it illustrates the point usefully.

all part of the basic transaction – but people might object if the garage tipped off a tyre and battery subsidiary to ring up and try to sell a new set, which is not related to the original transaction.

In practice it becomes increasingly hard to understand what 'confidentiality' should mean in a particular situation, particularly with large, complex and interlinked organisations like DSS:

- Who in fact is 'you'? The officer you gave the information to? The office they work in? The agency? DSS? Government? The public sector?
- So at what point could 'you' be said to pass PI on to 'someone else', and therefore violate confidentiality?

However, the fact that the bounds of confidentiality are getting harder to define does not mean it no longer matters – on the contrary, the more people suspect that information travels about the more they want to be reassured that confidentiality is respected and safeguarded. They still want the basic principle of confidentiality to apply, even though the details of who should be entitled to have access to it may not be obvious or explicit.

Participants did not usually have a clear view about how this should operate, apart from wanting to be told more about how the information would be used and by whom. Again, they typically have little clue about the internal structures of DSS (or any other large organisations), so they cannot propose specific rules about who can and who can't see or use their PI.

I have distilled the following general principles[10], which I think would command widespread support among my participants, although their components usually only emerged in a piecemeal and partial fashion from the interviews, for the reasons given above.

a) Personal information is handed over *for a purpose*. The purpose legitimises the demand for information – which people might otherwise not want to provide.

b) Among other reasons for reluctance in supplying personal information is the sense that this violates personal privacy (see 4.1.7) – but the sense of

10 These are generally congruent with the Data Protection Registrar's principles, but they reach further into matters like who should have access to data. Moreover the DPR's principle 3 says that disclosure should not be 'incompatible' with purpose, but I believe the public would want to go further to say that disclosure should not take place unless *justified* by purpose. I also find the concept of 'transaction' helpful – purposes are often very general, but transactions are usually more specific, which accords with the way the public tend to see matters.

violation is minimised if the PI is *only seen and handled by duly-appointed professionals* who are:

- 'licensed' to receive it
- dispassionate and anonymous
- trusted to keep confidence and use the information fairly and legitimately.

These 'licensed' professionals are analogous in role to a doctor, priest or bank manager, all of whom may safely be told certain things no-one else is allowed to know.

c) The provision of personal information is usually related to a *fairly specific and definable transaction* or set of transactions:

- whether asking or applying for something (like a benefit, a service, a product, a passport, a licence etc)
- or simply providing information required by the state or requested by other bodies (like tax returns, census or electoral registration forms, surveys, etc).

d) In principle one could imagine a *box* round the transaction:

- the information is put in the box
- it is seen only by people who legitimately operate within the box (and are 'licensed' to do so)
- collection and use of the information is defined and limited by the purpose of the transaction.

e) If information then travels *out of the box* (to different people or for different purposes) this potentially violates confidentiality – which should not happen without

- a compelling reason (valid and serious)
- an appropriate level of control and perhaps authorisation
- consulting (or at least informing) the person concerned – either by warning them in advance or telling them at the time of disclosure (and ideally by asking their permission).

F: 'It's something you've given to one department[11], you expect it to stay in that department because it's for a specific reason. I don't like to think that somebody else could check up on me with a certain department'

(Mid, low-TEA, 45–64)

---

11 It is not clear whether or not this refers to *government* departments.

M: 'I think they're entitled to have this information, but I don't think it should be spread around, it should be kept localised'

(Nth, benefits, 60+)

F: 'If you give information to one body you don't expect it to be passed about. If I told you something about me, would I expect you to go and tell your neighbour tomorrow? You're telling one governing body something about yourself and yet it can be passed about – which is wrong'

(Nth, 16–34)

I: 'Does it bother you the feeling that officials will be looking at details of your private life?'
F: 'No because that's their job'

(Mid, graduates, 35–44)

A transaction-based concept of confidentiality is useful because it allows data to follow pathways which are efficient for the customer (see 4.2.2.1) without opening licence for wider disclosure.

The *'transaction box'* is not necessarily defined by geographical or even organisational boundaries. If only one part of an organisation is legitimately involved in a transaction then other parts of the same organisation should not be entitled to know about it. Conversely, a given transaction may involve more than one organisation – for example the administration of Housing Benefit or Unemployment Benefit, or multi-supplier deals in the private sector. In those circumstances the transaction may justify certain kinds of relevant information being passed from one organisation to other – but *only* to those legitimately involved in the transaction on either side.

The concept of the 'purpose' of the transaction is central to the above analysis. It is also central to the DPR's principles, but there it seems broader and more general in scope – organisations register 'purposes', and must act in conformity with those purposes. Participants were concerned with the purposes of the *transaction* as well as the purposes of the *organisation* – something they might see as legitimate in a general way for the organisation may not seem a legitimate part of a particular transaction. A large organisation (certainly one as ramified as DSS) registers a very large number of 'purposes', many of which would lie far from a particular transaction. The public's perception tends to be that information is given for an immediate purpose, and perhaps for related purposes arising directly from that. The DPA stance can seem to imply that as long as both the purpose and the person to whom data is disclosed are registered then the disclosure is in order. The DSS DPA registrations run to many pages, cover a multiplicity of purposes (and would probably seem impenetrable to most members of the public).

Raymond Wacks writes (*Personal Information: Privacy and the Law,* p195f), "An associated problem concerns data which, although obtained or collected for one purpose, are used for another. This is normally a data-usage problem ... but may arise at the collection stage as well, since information may willingly be given on the understanding that it is to be used for a specific purpose only. Consent may therefore extend only to that use; had the data subject been informed that the data were to be disclosed or transferred to some other agency, his original consent to their collection might have been withheld ... An individual cannot be expected to be consenting to uses of data he supplies if he is unaware of what these uses are. The Government's White Paper, *Computers and Privacy* recognised that 'people asked to provide information should have a right to know for what purposes it will be used, and who is likely to have access to it'".

An article in *Personal Data Protection in Health and Social Services* (Penelope Pearce *et al*, Croom Helm 1988) discusses disclosure practice in the Social Services context. Having said that "this question of purpose is perhaps the most important of all the Principles", they argue (p70) that it is important to distinguish between disclosure for social services purposes, and disclosure for the purposes of those to whom it is made. In the former case it should be based on the written consent of the subject, "except where the service and resource necessarily and clearly involves such disclosure". In the latter case there is a specific departmental list of people who may be allowed disclosure for their own purposes.

4.1.7 Why people prize confidentiality

Why do most people seem to value confidentiality? In general they do so because it gives them some control over who gets access to information about them. As James Michael in *Privacy and Human Rights* (p3) puts it, "What we claim is that others should not obtain *knowledge* about us without our consent. In Professor Westin's words, this is 'the claim of individuals, groups or institutions to determine when, how, and to what extent information about them is communicated to others'".

So long as information remains confidential to the people we directly give it to we retain some control of this kind, but if they pass it on to third parties without our knowledge and consent we lose control – and even more so if those third parties may in turn pass it on to a multitude of other parties, as computer technology now makes routinely possible.

A few participants argued that unwillingness to disclose PI can affect other people (directly or indirectly), so a balance has to be struck between the need to give individuals as much control as possible over their PI, and the need society may sometimes have to insist that they do divulge it.

> *F: 'But there are other situations where it affects other people if you don't give out this information. So if it does affect other people then you have to question, well in whose best interest is it? It's got to be some kind of court to decide'*
>
> (Lon, lone parent, 16–29)

There seem to be three main classes of reason[12] why control of PI is important to us:

a) Protection of personal interests: One reason why people want to monitor and control others' use of their PI is simply to protect their own interests. Where people have 'something to hide' because they are behaving illegitimately or have supplied false or materially incomplete information they naturally have an interest in protecting their own situation. But someone who is scrupulously honest in their dealings may still feel threatened by uncontrolled disclosure of information about them – for example:

- Possession of personal information may give the person who knows power over the person who is known – if others have information about you they may use it to your disadvantage (whether deliberately or incidentally).
- Wrong, misleading or incomplete information could in any case damage you or work against your interest even if no-one is actively trying to manipulate you – it might reduce your chances of getting a job (or a loan, or a benefit), for example, perhaps without your even knowing.

b) Protection of privacy: Much has been written (for example Raymond Wacks, *op cit*) about the difficulties of making a satisfactory legal definition of 'privacy'[13], but there is no doubt from this research that it is a live and important concern to most people, however diffuse it may be as a legal concept.

Colin Bennett (*Regulating Privacy*, p23) says: "The concern is essentially to protect or promote the dignity, individuality, integrity or private personality of each one of us. The promotion of this value bolsters John Stuart Mill's basic principle of a liberal society that 'over himself, over his own body and mind, the individual is sovereign'".

Most people have a strong sense that they are entitled to personal space which is not wantonly invaded by the rest of society. Information about who they are, what they do, what they have or how they think is part of their personal lives, and should not be made available to other people except by themselves – at their own discretion and under their control. It is 'not their business' – they 'don't need to know'.

---

12 These categories come out of my research, but Colin J Bennett also uses three similar categories on p22 of his book *Regulating Privacy* – his titles are 'humanistic', 'instrumental' and 'political'.

13 'Privacy' goes much wider than PI – it includes topics like surveillance, media intrusion etc.

F: 'There's things that are just private to you. Anything related to me, it is up to me who I want to tell'

F: 'And having told one person, you don't want to feel that the world's going to know'

F: 'I don't expect them to tell somebody. It's my information, I own it'

(Sth, mid-TEA, 45–64)

M: 'It's part of our human culture – you need to retain something that's personal, something of your own that's yours to cling on to. Knowledge about you or your being or your circumstances or whatever it is, some people just feel the need that some parts of that they wanna keep private – it's just probably a human psychological thing'

(Sth, graduates, 35–44)

This applies even if they do not stand to be objectively harmed by disclosure – another reason why the 'If you've nothing to hide...' maxim has limited validity. As James Michael says (*Privacy & Human Rights*, p2), "This widespread, if not universal, desire for privacy is not limited to activities – or information about them – which would necessarily lead to unpleasant consequences, or produce guilt or shame in the person concerned".

F: 'I've got nothing to hide, but what I do in my life's my business, nothing to do with Mrs Jones sat over there, or anybody else's business. I don't go and pry into their lives. I wouldn't dream of telling people about my life'

(Nth, 16–34)

M: 'Well it isn't always right for someone else to want to know the whys and wherefores of you, even if you have got nothing to hide'

(Nth, benefits, 65+)

Some feel that personal privacy is progressively being eroded.

M: 'I think people are entitled to certain privacy. I don't think we've got any privacy now. I think it's like Big Brother. Well they've put it down to progress haven't they, modern technology?'

(Mid, benefits, 45–64)

c) Protection of society: The preceding two categories are both concerned with the specific effects of disclosure on the individuals concerned (and perhaps their families or immediate contacts). But some people have more systemic concerns. Since knowledge is seen to carry power it is sometimes argued that a significant increase in State information about individuals would tip the balance of power towards the State and away from the citizen. 'Big Brother' is the most potent and pervasive symbol of this fear. One of the traditions of British democracy has been that the state allows space to its citizens – it does not routinely keep tabs on what they are doing, assumes they are innocent until proved guilty, and generally lets them get on with their lives unless there is a specific and important public interest reason for interfering.

> *M: 'The more information you've got about people, it tends to give you a greater power over those people, and I think when you start pooling it all together, suddenly the police have powers which maybe they hadn't ought to have. You might start saying, well, there are certain groups of people within the community that commit most crimes, so we'll now start looking at all those that earn a certain amount of money, and therefore we can find out where they are – and you start using the power that you've got because of the information you've got in the wrong way. It gives them far too much power'*
>
> (Mid, graduates, 35–44)

> *F: 'Well they say Big Brother's watching you don't they, I mean they've got that much information about every single one of us – and it's just a fact and I don't think you can escape from it these days. There should be certain things that remain sacred, but there don't appear to be'*
>
> (Nth, benefits, 40+)

Confidentiality in personal information is sometimes argued to be important on these more general grounds – protecting individual freedoms by limiting overall state information about individuals, and keeping that information compartmentalised so that Departments only know what they need to know to carry out their own business.

Some feel that highly centralised government information might facilitate (if not encourage) centralisation of power, and perhaps lead to more state control over individuals than most people would like to see. Information which may seem fairly innocuous in normal circumstances (like ethnic origin) might become lethal if an intolerant government came to power. Many people (often including those who say they have nothing to hide) become nervous at the thought that their doings and their particulars might be logged and monitored in some central government database (see 4.2.2.2).

> *F: 'I'm just uncomfortable with it, you talk as if it's always going to be a benevolent government that's going to do all these things. Well I think you've got to try and keep it in control in case it isn't. Again going back to say Nazi Germany, they might want to know things about you that would be quite unreasonable – and one needn't think that it's never gonna happen just because it never has, it easily could'*
>
> (Sth, graduates, 35–44)

Colin Bennett (*Regulating Privacy*, p29) writes that "information technology could become a tool of tyranny. From the classic liberal belief in limited government springs a distrust of the effects of power. Information technology enhances the power of government to collect and manipulate vast quantities of information about individual citizens – an intrinsic cause for concern".

Systemic concerns seem fairly widespread at the level of generalised 'Big Brother' imagery, but not many people made a more developed systemic critique. More educated people seemed more likely to talk of these things, but most participants remained mainly focused on the implications for individuals. However, there was usually a body of agreement with such points when they were made.

4.1.8 Information technology

Many people blame problems with PI on computers. However, as Colin Bennett points out (*op cit* p17) it is the development of telecommunications and networks allied to the spread of computers which has brought about the major change: "Instantaneous access to vast qualities of information from multiple and remote locations has changed the character of the modern organisation and of the society in which it is embedded. This change is probably more a revolution in the nature of communication than in the nature of information itself. Paul Sieghart (*Privacy and Computers*, Latimer 1976) describes the information society as follows:

> 'More transactions will tend to be recorded; the records will tend to be kept longer; information will tend to be given to more people; more data will tend to be transmitted over public communication channels; fewer people will know what is happening to the data; the data will tend to be more easily accessible; and data can be manipulated, combined, correlated, associated and analysed to yield information which could not have been obtained without the use of computers' ".

The 20-year-old embedded quotation from Sieghart seems to have been prescient – the factors he identified seem the main sources of the concerns reflected in the present study.

4.1.8.1 Image of manual systems

Manual filing systems were seen to have their own confidentiality problems. They were prone to obvious leakage – eg left around on desks, open to prying eyes, perhaps visible to cleaners or other unauthorised personnel. This is what some people envisaged as they looked across service counters and saw papers and files on desks and in filing trays. For some older people this is still the most obvious threat they see – it is a tangible risk, you can visualise it happening. However it generally seems a fairly contained kind of potential damage, because the number of people who might get to see it would probably be very limited. Indeed the image of manual systems implies a certain degree of protection for PI from the nature of the process:

- seemingly fairly inaccessible – you'd need to be on the spot, you couldn't get at it from a distance

- difficult to extract large quantities of information – it would have to be done by copying papers
- probably limited in life – because of storage problems the material would probably be periodically destroyed.

Manual files are also thought likely to get lost, which can be frustrating.

4.1.8.2 Image of computerised systems

Most people have a fairly vivid image of computers – but this is often hazy and sometimes inaccurate.

Computer data is widely seen:

- to be voluminous in quantity – computers can hold more information about individuals than is practical with manual records, and can store it for longer and in larger quantity
- to facilitate rapid access and retrieval, even from remote sites
- to enable broader or deeper analysis of information to be made – including cross-checks between different databanks
- to make sharing or pooling of PI easier – through networking, 'tapping in', mass transfer of data, and so on
- to make more data available about each person – and in more usable form
- to be more prone to error – including larger-scale errors, since some people argue that a random error in a manual file is likely to cause only limited damage, whereas a computer error could have major and widespread repercussions
- to be less safe and secure – because computers allow wider-scale access (whether licit or illicit), and because people have heard stories about networks, the Internet, 'hackers' and so on.

F: 'Computers I think are worse'
M: 'Anybody can get into a computer if they really want to, can't they?'
F: 'If it's in a file in an office then they have to go to that office and that particular drawer and take it out'
F: 'Well they can read it lying on somebody's desk, but it's usually only one other person that's looking at it – but with a computer anybody can lock into a computer'

(Mid, low-TEA, 45–64)

M: 'If you have a file then you have to physically go to that file to look –'
F: 'And people won't bother'
M: 'So if I want to find out something about you I would have to go and search that about you. But if it was on computer, I could do that from anywhere – anywhere in the world'

(Lon, benefits, 16–39)

M: 'I think information on computers is a lot more dangerous because it's so easy to copy, and to find the indexing is so easy. I think the paperwork part of things is going out the window gradually and I don't think there'll be too much on paper before too long. The databases are so comprehensive, there's so many headings you can have and there's so many cross-referencing facilities in it that anything they can get stays there. It's so easy to keep now, not like on paper'

(Sth, benefits, 30–44)

M: 'Errors on a piece of paper are analogue, it's a letter, you can say, "Oh it's a spelling mistake", but if you make a mistake on a computer, press number 3 instead of 6, it'll come up with something completely different, it'll give you an AIDS test instead of an eye test'

(Sth, mid-TEA, 45–64)

It seems generally assumed that the same pattern will go on developing, with computers getting more universally used, more powerful, more inter-linked – and holding ever more personal information. Hence any threats perceived in the present set-up are expected to intensify in future.

M: 'If you look at all the junk mail that comes through it's all got a reference number on, so we're not a name, you are getting a number, that somebody somewhere can punch that number into a computer and they can tell when I used the car to get some petrol, or if I've been to Argos, or whatever I've done, they can tell. If I went off last weekend to Blackpool and I stopped overnight and used me credit card they can tell. There's nothing that we can do to stop it'

(Nth, benefits, 40+)

Many people are very hazy about how computers and networks actually work in practice, which can cause them either to exaggerate or to underestimate the problems. Some seem to overestimate the universality of access – a few imagine that 'anyone with a computer' can get at more or less anything, which probably comes from a fusion of half-digested news-stories about networks, hacking, the Internet etc.

M: 'I know there's modern technology and all this, but how the hell did they know my address, I've never dealt with them before in my life. All right they go through like computers I suppose, but what else can they do with these computers?'

(Mid, benefits, 45–64)

F: 'Anyone with the Internet can hack into other people's numbers and find out all sorts of information about them'
I: 'Do you think that outsiders can hack into DSS computers?'
M: 'Yes'
F: 'It's been known that it happens'
M: 'Yeah, if they can hack into like American defence computers they can get into the DSS'
I: 'Do you think this is a live enough possibility for you to be concerned about personally?'

M: 'Yes. This is all new, like you can access any information in the whole world, no-one's ever been here before, that's why it scares people. Well there's no laws on the Internet to control anything, and information's the most valuable commodity in the world – of course we're scared. The technology is expanding beyond any responsibility in how to use it correctly, and we don't know what the hell's going on'

(Lon, benefits, 16–39)

Elderly people often seem most bemused by IT and computers. A minority of office workers seemed to have more grasp of networks and file transfer – but real understanding was rare in most sectors.

4.2 Using and disclosing PI

Having considered general attitudes and concerns about PI and confidentiality we now look at various aspects of using and disclosing personal information.

4.2.1 Possible data relationships

Different bodies or individuals who possess PI can have different levels of data-sharing relationship. I got a sense of this from the early interviews, and devised the following piece of stimulus material for use in the remaining sessions.

Common information, totally shared
Unrestricted access to other database
Freely available on request
Available on request for good reason
Needs special permission
Needs legal process
Not available under any circumstances

This generally worked well, and helped people focus their ideas about the basis on which different kinds of information should (or should not) be passed between different bodies. Participants seemed to understand the concept – and liked the sense of structure and control it implies. The ideas which flowed from it are discussed in 4.2.4.2 and 4.3.5.

4.2.2 Sharing and pooling information

Increasing the level of data-sharing has potential advantages and disadvantages.

4.2.2.1 Advantages of more data sharing

Some people think more sharing of personal information might be beneficial to the public:

- either in terms of direct potential advantages for the individual
- or because it helps make things more efficient if the system works better.

However, such advantages are certainly not always obvious – few people came up spontaneously with advantages, even when asked if they could see any possible benefits in increased availability of information.

The main potential advantages suggested (mostly by small minorities) were:

a) More efficient for customers: For example:

- If PI can be remotely accessed then information will be available when and where it is needed:
  - when away from the home area
  - in cases of accident and emergency
- Service delivery may be speeded up or improved
- Efficient 'recycling' of PI could reduce form-filling – many information needs might be met from stock rather than continually having to ask for more data
- If fuller use can be made of PI then it becomes easier to get the right help to people:
  - entitlement to benefits could be more proactively assessed – telling you what you're entitled to rather that waiting for you to claim it
  - people in need of help could be more easily identified – perhaps on a cross-agency basis.

F: 'Sometimes you give one lot of information to one department and it would be just as easy if they passed it round a bit, but they don't'
I: 'You find yourself being asked the same things time and time again?'
F: 'Over and over again. Well things like the fact that I am divorced, and they always want to know when your husband left and how long you have been single and all that sort of thing, whereas if that sort of record was held by – . Well it is usually people like the DHSS, and I deal with the Child Support Agency, and they don't share with each other'
I: 'And you think they should?'
F: 'Well I think because they are all working for the benefit of us in the long run. And I would think it would help them if they knew what they were doing'

(Sth, benefits, 45–64)

M: 'It would make our lives more efficient and easy if it was being used positively in our interests'

(Lon, benefits, 16–39)

M: 'If there was an efficient system in situ then you could maybe get a situation where you're actually being told that you're entitled to something rather than having to find out by a longwinded set of form filling'

F: 'If they're linked together you should only need to give the information once'

(Mid, graduates, 35–44)

F: 'They probably get their claims or whatever through quicker because the information's already there, and they haven't got to go through the rigmarole of going through all the information separately again'

(Mid, lone parent, 30–44)

b) More efficient for the system: Data made more available can be more productively used:

- Things might work more smoothly, efficiently or economically
- Abuse can be reduced, and fraud and crime more effectively detected.

M: 'I think there's an atmosphere of mutual distrust here, like we don't wanna give the authorities the information – but if we did, that might speed up the system, and make everything a little bit smoother, and stop the queues or whatever. I mean if there was an ideal relationship we'd give as much information as possible, all on computer, it'd all be on line'

(Lon, benefits, 16–39)

F: 'There's advantages when you look at the criminal side obviously because when information is pooled then it would be a lot quicker sometimes to find out all the information that they need'

(Mid, graduates, 35–44)

M: 'If it's going to help 'em get anybody who's doing something really serious then it's a bonus really'

(Sth, benefits, 30–44)

These potential advantages would be welcome and valued:

- Although people want confidentiality they tend to get irritated if they are delayed or inconvenienced because their PI is not in the right place at the right time
- Being able to walk into any branch office and get rapid action on your account is desirable
- Having fewer or smaller forms to fill in would certainly be widely appreciated
- People often resent the fact that entitlements are not pointed out to them
- Many people would like to see serious fraud or crime reduced – partly on principle, because it is unfair that others should profit from wrong-doing; and partly because they feel honest people end up paying for criminal acts – either because they have to foot the bill as taxpayers, or because it reduces the pot of benefit money available to those who are really entitled to it.

However, even when advantages like the above were suggested they were often received sceptically:

i) The government machine is not widely seen to *want* to act proactively in volunteering help which is not actually claimed – especially not the Social Security system. This is often thought to be inhibited more by government attitudes than by over-restricted access to personal information.

ii) Computerisation to date seems to have produced more and longer forms, not less.

iii) While many would like to see serious fraud stamped on they often suspect that an information-based clampdown would not actually work – 'honest' people might find life more difficult and inquisitorial while 'villains' continued to get away with things.

M: 'They never pass anything on that's good for you, they don't work that way, they're trying to stop everybody from getting – '

(Mid, benefits, 45–64)

M: 'I think if that sort of (centralised) system worked well it would make life easier for everybody, you would know that your valid information was always up-to-date rather than hanging about in an office in an in-tray that could be there for months and months, or we've lost your records, things we've all heard before'
F: ' "Can you fill in another form?" '
F: 'But don't you think that would happen anyway, what makes you think that that won't happen, it won't all hang about on some bit of the computer it can't reach. It still depends on people'
M: 'No I don't think that would happen, with the technology we're talking about that shouldn't happen'
F: 'And also it'll be entered incorrectly, it'll be just as much of a balls-up as ever'

(Sth, graduates, 35–44)

4.2.2.2 Disadvantages of more data sharing

While not many people are convinced of the possible advantages to freer data-sharing most are more aware of the potential drawbacks –

- It becomes harder to control access or use of your PI, or to get any real picture of who is using it for what purposes
- 'Confidentiality' becomes harder to define or establish
- If a wide range of government departments (and other bodies) can 'tap in' to your information, people who 'have no business to' may 'look at your particulars'
- The more people that have access the greater the apparent risk of leaks or misuse

- Centralised information could be particularly dangerous – wrong, out-of-date or misleading information could then blight large areas of someone's life.

M: 'There is another aspect of the idea of hacking into systems and things, once information is centralised and pooled, then if undesirables get hold of that information they could use it for all sorts of purposes that you wouldn't want'

(Mid, graduates, 35–44)

M: 'As long as there's some safeguards. I don't think we should have an open book on all information, because that then leads to people just having a look, "Oh I wonder what so-and-so's doing?", and looking up their neighbour, or this type of thing'

(Sth, mid-TEA, 45–64)

M: 'What I would be saying about freedom of information in a pool is that you've lost total control, and that's just a bit of control I like to retain'
F: 'I don't think you've got much control anyway'

(Sth, graduates, 35–44)

M: 'It would certainly make it catastrophic if they made a mistake, if it was totally centralised. It could totally destroy your life'
F: 'And then you're guilty before you're proven innocent rather than the other way round'
M: 'So I hope that doesn't happen – well I hope it doesn't exist at the moment. I don't think it does. I don't believe so'
F: 'And also centralisation of a great deal of information means if somebody was to tamper with it they would get more information, they would get everything about you in one go rather than one little bit. So that's then even more dangerous isn't it?'

(Sth, mid-TEA, 45–64)

Amalgamating and cross-relating information from many sources could provide an uncomfortably vivid and detailed picture of an individual. This is often seen as:

- an invasion of privacy
- a potential instrument of state control.

M: 'I don't worry about what individual organisations know, it's just when the entire picture is combined from all what they know, trading information backwards and forwards between them, they might get an overall picture which I wouldn't be too keen on them having. I'm pretty sure it does happen'

(Lon, benefits, 16–39)

M: 'I mean the government knows how much you earn, they know where you work, how much you're paid, how many kids you've got – they know so much about you. How much you've got in the bank, they know everything, what car you've got, where you live'

(Mid, low-TEA, 45–64)

James Michael in *Privacy and Human Rights* says (p10): "It is now possible to construct a profile of a person which may be considered to be invasive of privacy from individual items of information which would *not* be considered 'private and personal' .... the widespread use of personal computers and the existence of distributed data banks linked by public communications networks makes it possible, at least in principle, for many people to gain access to such profiles".

Again, centralising of information may also make the state too powerful vis-à-vis the individual – references to 'Big Brother' were quite often heard.

> *M: 'During the Gulf War they were very quickly able to round up every single Iraqi or Iraqi origin person who was living in the country. Now clearly they have a highly centralised and effective information network on people's ethnic origins, which I think is downright sinister. And what with deportations at the moment I think that it's extremely nasty stuff potentially'*
>
> (Mid, graduates, 35–44)

Colin Bennett (*Regulating privacy,* p40) quotes the British Younger Committee's 1972 survey, in which 87% thought that recording personal details on a large central government databank would be 'an invasion of privacy', 71% said they would be 'very annoyed or upset' about this, and 85% thought such databanks should be prohibited by law. This information is now dated, but my research provides no reason to suppose that these attitudes have changed radically.

Raymond Wacks writes in 1989 (*Personal Information: Privacy and the Law,* p178) "Already there are alarming signs that the drift towards centralised databanks is inexorably posing disturbing threats to individual freedom. And there can be little doubt that, in the absence of clearly formulated legal controls, we are in serious danger of creating an automated, authoritarian society from which there is no escape". Having warned against overstating "Dystopian versions of Big Brother" he nevertheless concludes that "in Britain and elsewhere there are increasing signs of serious abuses committed in the name of efficiency".

He further writes (p203f): "Foremost amongst the fears of those who prognosticate the future of life with (or under) computers is that of a large centralised data bank which, facilitated by a universal personal identifier (UPI), is able to synthesize data from a variety of sources. These fears are not easily allayed by assurances from the Government that no such plan is under consideration. The process may be taking place in a gradual, almost imperceptible manner". He refers to:

- the "merging of the data banks of the DHSS and the Departments of Inland Revenue and Employment"

- "a disturbing trend toward granting the Inland Revenue and perhaps other government departments the power to gain access to the centralised DHSS network"
- use of 'DHSS' data for tracing purposes by the police and MI5.

Jabire and DeWolf write on p8 of *Private Lives and Public Policies*, a 1993 report from the Panel on Confidentiality and Data Access to the US Committee on National Statistics and the Social Research Council: "Many citizens believe increasingly and with some justification that their privacy is being eroded by organisations that develop and control the use of large data bases that contain detailed information about them. They see linkage of data from different sources as a particular threat. For these and other reasons, statistical agencies are finding it more difficult to persuade persons and organisations to participate in statistical surveys, whether voluntary or mandatory".

Some participants argued that a government's desire to centralise information would imply a breakdown in the basic view that individuals are normally trusted to report their own circumstances – subject of course to investigation in cases of doubt, but basically assumed 'innocent until proved guilty'.

> *M: 'It's taking everything away from the honesty of the individual, and I think some things have got to be left to be down to the person to say, "Yes I am", and there shouldn't have to be 100% proof about everything'*
>
> (Sth, benefits, 30–44)

> *M: 'Stick to the old adage that you're innocent until proved guilty, so I think the fact that you could link those two computers together and always have access is unnecessary. I think it's something where if there are grounds for checking up on somebody or there's a suspicion then the information would be made available'*
>
> (Mid, graduates, 35–44)

Finally, people often feel pressured and mistrusted if their every action seems documented and collated – again this is still often true if they feel they have 'nothing to hide'. The more honest and respectable the citizen, the more wounding it can be to feel suspected.

> *M: 'If it was centralised and there was no control over what, there was no seriousness factor involved and they could just jump on you willy-nilly whenever they wanted to, it would worry me, and I'd be afraid to go out the front door. But if I knew that there's still certain freedom left and you knew those limits – I don't think life would be worth living if you couldn't sort of do anything'*
>
> (Sth, benefits, 30–44)

4.2.3 Reliability

Various concerns relate to what we might call reliability in relation to PI. These divide into two main types, relating to *accuracy* and to *security*.

4.2.3.1 Accuracy of information

How far is PI information correct? And is it up-to-date? People often fear that information which is wrong, or misleading, or which no longer applies, could be harmful.

F: 'Given that every other day you read something in the papers about Fraud Squads and things and you're aware of this completely kind of Neanderthal operation which is constantly making huge errors – I certainly sometimes have nightmares of my name appearing on some screen somewhere, or if someone saw a piece of paper (wrongly) saying three people lived in that house and she put in an application saying one person lived in this house, for all she knew there could be a fraud investigation'

(Lon, benefits, 16–39)

F: 'It's almost like having the power to control you, somebody's got all this information about you and they can control you if you don't do as they say'
M: 'Yeah and it might not even be correct information or relevant information'
F: 'Exactly. Or they can change it'

(Mid, graduates, 35–44)

F: 'The information isn't always correct that they're passing around – well at some point a mistake has been made, that is then being passed round to several other people who haven't checked it, and they're just using it'

(Sth, mid-TEA, 45–64)

These fears are often fuelled by stories (or sometimes actual experiences) of credit rating agencies which have blacklisted people because there are incorrect records of past debts (arising for example from successfully disputed bills, computer errors in invoices or arrears notices, mistaken identity etc), or records of debts which have long since been paid. They assume such errors could occur in other kinds of data.

F: 'I have a friend at the moment who is fighting a case because somebody said she has got a County Court judgement against her – and she has not, but it is down on her – and that could be detrimental to her if she wanted to take something up'

(Sth, benefits, 45–64)

F: 'That happened to my neighbour – they said her name was blacklisted, and when she checked up it was the water board, she'd paid the bill but for some reason, a mistake on a computer, she'd got blacklisted – and it's all been rectified now but she had to go through all that'

(Nth, benefits, 40+)

F: 'When your home gets black-listed the address is black-listed when you move into it. It's the address that's black-listed, not the person'

(Lon, benefits, 16–39)

M: 'My son's had a conviction, it can stop me getting credit 'cos he lives at my address, I mean this is ridiculous'

(Nth, benefits, 40+)

Computers (or rather their operators) are seen to be fairly error-prone – and small computer errors can sometimes have large effects (see 4.1.8.2).

People fear that information might be misleading even if not actually wrong – it might be incomplete, or decision-makers might just draw on the database instead of talking to the person concerned.

F: 'It might be misinterpreted'
M: 'Any type of information taken out of context could well be damaging'
(Sth, mid-TEA, 45–64)

In some ways people approve of information being kept for future use – it would be irritating and inefficient to have to keep collecting everything from scratch. But stored information can easily date, since people's circumstances sometimes change rapidly. They feel that it needs to be updated, or verified before use – but are not confident this always happens, particularly when passed on to other organisations.

4.2.3.2 Security of information

People simply do not know how much potential there is for unauthorised access – for information to leak out, or to be seen or used in illegitimate ways. This is often a concern:

- Computers have a fairly 'leaky' image – largely because of stories about 'hacking' and networking (see 4.1.8.2).
- Managers or staff on the ground in a large organisation may not always follow organisational policies or observe safeguards and procedures. They may be careless – or even venial, since PI is now beginning to be seen as a commercially valuable commodity. Staff turnover or disaffection may also be a threat.

M: 'You should also have an expectation of that stuff to be kept in certain locked confidential files and so on. I've seen examples of where people have found confidential files lying around on desks all over the place, where you expect stuff to be confidential. If the filing cabinet is open, and anybody can get to it then of course it isn't confidential, even though it may say on it "Confidential file"'
(Mid, graduates, 35–44)

M: 'No matter what systems you put in place and what legislation is passed by government, if there are humans operating the systems there are always going to be humans that are open to abusing the systems'
(Lon, benefits, 16–39)

F: 'You're relying on the integrity of the employees really, because there can be an act or a law but if somebody wants to break that law'
I: 'On the whole, as far as government departments are concerned, do you feel you can trust the integrity of the employees or not?'
M: 'They're basically the same as everybody else'
(Sth, mid-TEA, 45–64)

F: 'There was a court case a couple of weeks ago and it was a woman who actually worked at the DSS herself, and she hated this other female so much, so she used all this information about this woman that she got, everything about where she banked, her finances, and she just made this woman's life hell for about 18 months'

(Nth, benefits, 40+)

Security is a concern in the NHS as well as DSS. An article by Chris Wills on p189 of the *Health Libraries Review* (1985) says "Members of the public are increasingly concerned about the physical safety of personal records. There have been cases of filing cabinets left permanently unlocked, notes left to scatter along the street, and members of staff talking about patients in public places. All of this is to be deplored and steps should be taken to ensure that all staff are aware of and practice the procedures relating to the security of patient/client records".

Jabire and De Wolf (*op cit*) recommend (p7) that "There should be legal sanctions for all users, both external users and agency employees, who violate requirements to maintain the confidentiality of data", and (p12) that agencies "should take steps to provide staff training in fair information practices, informed consent procedures, confidentiality laws and policies, statistical disclosure limitation procedures, and related topics".

4.2.3.3 'Soft' data

Some participants expressed concern about 'soft' data – including impressions, comments or opinions recorded by staff about individuals. These could be damaging, and may or may not be correct or justifiable.

4.2.4 Safeguards and protection

Most people think there should be safeguards about the use of PI – but don't feel they see much evidence that this is the case. It feels like a bit of a free-for-all, and most don't assume that anyone is doing much to protect the individual's interests in these matters.

4.2.4.1 Data Protection Act (DPA)

Quite a few participants seemed at least vaguely aware of the DPA[14], although a surprising number didn't seem to have heard of it at all, and very few knew much about it.

This is broadly in accord with recent evidence presented by the Data Protection Registrar (DPR). Appendix 5 of the DPR's 10th Annual Report gives the results of annual omnibus surveys, each based on a sample of about 1000 members of the general public. Results are given for 1992, '93 and '94. They suggest that:

- Only between a fifth and a quarter are 'aware that there is a law concerning rights about information kept on individuals'

14 No-one mentioned the Computer Misuse Act at all. I did not check for awareness.

- Only about 1 in 10 are spontaneously aware of the DPA
- When prompted for awareness of the DPA, about 1 in 5 say they have 'definitely heard of it', and about 1 in 8 'think so'
- Putting spontaneous and prompted awareness together, only about 2 in 5 are even vaguely aware of the Act
- Only 3–4% say they have 'ever made use of' the DPA
- There are few clear signs of trends in this information, although there was a significant increase in total awareness of the DPA in 1994 – but still not up to 50%.

The current research suggests that very few know what the Act actually says, even in broad terms – and some have misconceptions about it. Thus even the very modest levels of awareness seem to exaggerate the extent to which people really have a working knowledge of what the DPA does or could do for them as individual citizens.

> F: *'(DPA) If you hold things on computer you have to tell people, isn't it that? Don't you have to inform people that their records are held on computer?'*
> F: *'Yeah, and it cannot then be passed on to another organisation without that person's authority to do so'*
> F: *'We are a bit vague aren't we about the Data Protection Act?'*
>
> (Sth, mid-TEA, 45–64)

> F: *'The Data Protection Act does list quite a few things what they have to hold – the information is right in fact, and you can get it, and you can correct it if it's wrong'*
> M: *'And I think it does have something in it about transfer of data as well on to other databases. Isn't each data field or whatever they call them, each bit of data graded as being accessible or not? Like your name for example may be quite freely given but the National Insurance Number may not be'*
>
> (Mid, graduates, 35–44)

Subject access is probably the most commonly known provision – but it is still not widely understood. Awareness also tends to relate to particular examples rather than general rights – for example many people have heard they are now entitled to see their medical records, but do not necessarily relate this to the DPA, or assume it is part of a broader class of similar rights. Many assume (if they know or hear about the DPA) that it does not apply to government departments. Few people have tried to exercise subject access rights, and most are sceptical about their likely effectiveness or usefulness (see 4.2.5).

> M: *'I remember reading about the Data Protection Act and the fact that people have got records from now on about you, or who are starting to collect data bases on people, have to say what their records contain. But I've no idea really how to access that information from somewhere like the DHSS or the public sector'*

I: 'But do you know whether you have a right to it from the DSS or not?'
M: 'Well no, no, I don't know'

(Mid, graduates, 35–44)

On the whole the DPA seems to have a dilute and fairly ineffectual image, quite apart from not being widely known:

- most people are unaware of what it does
- they don't feel it has done much to allay their concerns
- and they wonder whether (and how) it is effectively policed.

M: 'Is there a body that goes round and kind of checks up on this, because you could write down all sorts of reasons for having data, and then use it for all sorts of other reasons?'

(Mid, graduates, 35–44)

4.2.4.2 Possible safeguards and controls

Some possible approaches to safeguards and controls for the use of PI were suggested.

a) Verification rather than disclosure: It is generally thought more permissible to verify that information another body already holds is correct, than to release information they don't already have. For example, many think it is less acceptable for DSS to tell an employer an employee's NI number than to confirm a number the employer already has[15].

b) 'Flagging': 'Flagging' rather than general disclosure was sometimes suggested if information has to be cross-checked with other databases – for example to check benefits against tax returns DSS need only tell IR which benefits individuals are claiming, and ask them to see whether this is consistent with their information. This avoids the need to exchange large quantities of PI, because the exchange is minimal unless inconsistencies are found. This would probably generally be preferred to large-scale disclosure – but would still be seen by many as a breach of confidence.

M: 'I think it's a good idea that if certain markers pop up to say this person has got so-and-so benefit, therefore he gets looked at by the Tax Office, and so there are certain connections but not total disclosure – because things like your shoe size is not of interest to the Tax Office, but it could be misconstrued, someone might dislike people with big feet'

(Sth, mid-TEA, 45–64)

---

15 It seems to me that verification could sometimes be less of a safeguard than many of my participants assume. A supposed verification request could sometimes be used to elicit new information – 'Can you confirm that Mr X is getting Income Support?' provides virtually the same information as the question 'Is Mr X getting Income Support?'. Nevertheless it remains a useful principle in suitable cases.

c) Access classification: Access to PI could be restricted on the basis of classification. It would be possible to classify different levels of staff and/ or different levels of information:

- Access classification for staff: Staff could be classified according to how far they should be allowed access to PI. This relates to people's notion that their personal information should only be available to those who are 'licensed' to see it by virtue of their function, and who are instructed and trained about keeping it confidential (see 4.1.6).
- Access classification for types of information: Highly sensitive information could be given extra protection – disclosure could be restricted to authorised recipients with high levels of access, and not made available to anyone else without special permission.

> *F: 'On your information there should be perhaps some sort of coding whereby if information is looked up on the screen there is a code next to items that weren't allowed to be released without permission'*
>
> (Sth, graduates, 35–44)

d) Gateways and procedures: I have suggested a spectrum of possibilities for controlling disclosure outside the transaction box (see 4.1.6), ranging from a common database, through various levels of authorisation to complete unavailability (see 4.2.1).

The public would like to feel that structured gateways and controls of this kind are applied to the movement of personal data – although unsure how far this is the case. The appropriate relationship depends on the nature of the bodies and the information involved, and on the transaction it relates to. Completely pooled data normally only seems acceptable between people dealing with the same transactions. Legal process (or at least high level authorisation) should be needed where the information or its pathway is particularly sensitive. Some of the main themes which affect DSS data are reviewed in 4.3.5.

> *F: 'They can't go into somebody's house without a warrant, so presumably they shouldn't be able to have access to information'*
>
> (Sth, graduates, 35–44)

e) Information and consultation: Many feel there should be a requirement at least to tell individuals if their information goes out of the transaction box – and preferably to consult them or ask their consent in important cases. This seems to them the fairest way to proceed – although clearly it could involve costs and practical difficulties if widely practised.

> *F: 'I don't think they should actually go into anything in your private life without telling you. Well I suppose it should be asking you, but under some circumstances they will actually do it by getting an order'*
>
> (Sth, benefits, 45–64)

F: 'I think that if they were to come to you and say, "We have been contacted by a particular department, they want information about you", that you should have a right to say, "I don't want you to disclose that information"'

(Sth, graduates, 35–44)

F: 'It's the fact that they're able to find this information on you without your permission. If they need to know that then they should come to me and then I will say, "Well yes you can have this information", or, "No I don't want to give it you"'

(Nth, 16–34)

F: 'I don't think there should be a bank of information about anybody unless that information's been given by you, and only you have the right to give permission to other organisations to draw that'

(Lon, lone parent, 16–29)

Explanation could either be provided in advance or only when a particular disclosure is due to take place. Telling people in advance what is likely to happen to their PI is the simplest procedure – further notification is then only needed if a disclosure is intended that is not within the scope of the original statement. But participants did not feel they are currently told what will happen to the information they provide – by DSS or most other bodies (see 4.1.3.2). Jabire and De Wolff (*op cit*) say on p9 that "The goal should be to give each data provider as much information as is necessary to make his or her consent as informed as he or she wishes it to be".

Some pointed out that asking consent could sometimes be a hollow process where people are dependent on an organisation – like DSS.

M: 'With your consent'
F: 'Then would there have been a threat that you wouldn't get the benefit unless you said yes?'
F: 'I wouldn't say I was so much giving them my consent as much as saying that I can't go for that job unless I give them that information'

(Sth, graduates, 35–44)

M: 'If you object to them finding out then obviously suspicion is thrown upon you and they'll stop your allowance just like that anyway'

(Mid, low-TEA, 45–64)

f) Better subject access: Most would like better and easier subject access – realistic ways of checking the scope and accuracy of records held about them (see 4.2.5).

g) Opt-outs: Some people remarked that commercial organisations put an opt-out tick-box on forms and questionnaires for people to use if they don't want their name passed on[16] – yet there is no similar facility to put limits on the uses of PI in the DSS (or general public sector) context.

h) PI agency: Some asked for an ombudsman or agency to police fair use of PI and adjudicate contentious cases. They either don't know about the Data Protection Registrar (as was often the case, see 4.2.4.1), or don't see the DPR in this role.

4.2.5 Subject access

Most people think they have a *moral right* to know what organisations have on file about them:

- it seems only fair that if people are holding your information you should be entitled to know what they have
- and in any case you should have a chance to make sure that the information is not actually wrong, out-of-date, or misleadingly incomplete – and to get it corrected.

I: 'Do you have a right to know what someone like the DSS has on file about you?'
F: 'I don't know if we do. I would like to know what they know, just to make sure that what they have got is what is true – because also circumstances change and they don't always up-date everything'

(Sth, benefits, 45–64)

Members of the public were asked in the Data Protection Registrar's omnibus survey (*op cit*) to say what importance they attached to various rights.

	1992	1993	1994
	%	%	%
Proportion saying the following rights are very important:			
To correct errors in information about yourself	83	84	83
To know what the information about you is being used for	80	80	81
To be told who the information about you is being passed to	83	83	81
To be told where the information about you came from	77	80	77
To see what information is held about you	77	79	77
To have yourself removed from lists or files	78	75	71
To add things to the information about yourself	68	69	65

All seven items get very high ratings – they are all rated 'very important' by between four fifths and two thirds of the sample. Over 80% say it is

16 Although some were sceptical about the efficacy of this.

very important to be able to correct errors, know what your information is used for, and know who has it. Again this suggests that disclosure to third parties without informing the subject is strongly disapproved of by the vast majority of the public. It also generally underlines the importance of clarifying how PI is used and handled.

However, the current research suggests that although most people feel they *should* have a right to see the information held about them, most are unsure:

- whether or how far they have enforceable *legal* rights
- what sort of rights they might have, or how to exercise them
- whether any such rights would apply to government departments.

> *F: 'Like with the DHSS, I reckon you should be able to see your own file'*
> *I: 'Can you, are you entitled to?'*
> *F: 'I don't know. This law did come out for something but I don't know whether you can or not now'*
> *I: 'What law was that?'*
> *F: 'Oh, that was the medical, you could see your own files'*
>
> (Mid, lone parent, 30–44)

Most people do not in practice feel they have meaningful subject access[17]. Many are unaware that they do have rights – or have at best a hazy and partial idea. There is fairly widespread awareness about the right to see their medical records, for example, but that is not often generalised to other types of PI. Awareness of the Data Protection Act is often very poor – and understanding is usually hazy at best (see 4.2.4.1).

> *M: 'Everybody's unsure of what their rights are when it comes to asking about information so we should be informed of what our rights are in terms of access, should be better informed, especially from the government'*
>
> (Mid, graduates, 35–44)

Most are doubtful whether any subject access rights they might have would apply to government departments – the general assumption is that they probably wouldn't. Few people really believe that they could insist on looking at their DSS or Inland Revenue records – particularly if there have been difficulties or disputes. If they do have rights in this area they don't feel they've been told about them – and wouldn't know how to go about exercising them.

---

17 'Subject access' is the DPA term for the individual's right to see their PI held on computer by a data user. This term was never used by participants, and I suspect it would not often be recognised or understood.

I: 'If you went along to a government department with proof of identity would they then be obliged to tell you what they know about you?'
M: 'I wouldn't think so for one minute, no'
F: 'I don't know, I thought the Data Protection Act – '
M: 'They ought to have to'

(Sth, graduates, 35–44)

M: 'As members of the public we don't know what is on computer about us. If I went down to the DSS and said, "Look, I wanna see what you have on computer about me", I'd be given a very short message – and probably the second word would be "off"'

(Lon, benefits, 16–39)

But even once they are told they have legal subject access rights which do apply to government departments as well as other public and private sector bodies people still do not tend to feel these really protect them. There seem to be a mass of practical problems and doubts which make subject-initiated access a doubtful way of regulating PI. Individuals' perceptions are often confused and fragmentary (although generally sceptical), but I have pieced together the following list of problems from what was said:

- There are *too many bodies* who might hold your PI. Access rights might be a way of dealing with a specific concern or a single manifest problem, but they are not much help if you are concerned about widespread transfer of information:
  - there might be hundreds (or thousands) of organisations who have your data
  - you may have no idea who has what.

  Subject access rights then become hard to enforce, even if known and understood.

- The *procedures are unclear* – and many people are unhappy about tangling with the authorities if they don't have to.

- Some people would be *nervous about asking to see their records* – this might cause trouble, you might find yourself labelled as a 'trouble-maker', or even victimised.

- There is fairly *widespread scepticism* about whether you would really get the truth:
  - records could be doctored or concealed for the purpose, and you would have no way of knowing
  - some people know the DPA doesn't cover manual records – and suspect there may be other exclusions.

M: 'The only problem with that is if they say, "All right leave it with us and we'll give it to you", they could delete half the stuff before they gave it to you anyway, or make a back-up of it'

(Sth, benefits, 30–44)

People don't know how far subject access is policed – and on the whole assume it probably isn't.

Very few participants had ever tried to access any of their records – although a minority had tried using 'mailing preference' facilities to cut down junk mail (with varying reported success).

4.2.6 *Different types of information*

I have used the term 'sensitive' to describe personal information which participants are particularly keen should be kept confidential. Not all PI is equally sensitive – sensitivity depends on two things:

a) Context-dependent factors: Information which might seem highly sensitive in one context may seem less so in another – again, things people would happily tell their doctor they might not want to say to their bank manager (and vice versa). It depends what information fits the situation, what seems appropriate, necessary and justified by the transaction and the context. People often said sensitivity depends on:

- who has it (or is asking for it)
- why they want it, and what they intend to do with it
- the situation or context of the transaction.

This is one of the problems with the increasing (and largely invisible) amount of data transfer between bodies – it is no longer possible to assess the 'who' and the 'why' if your PI ends up a long way from the box you originally thought you were putting it in (see 4.1.6).

b) Absolute factors: Although sensitivity may vary according to context, some types of information seem intrinsically likely to be more sensitive – eg medical and financial information. In principle it should be possible to classify information types by sensitivity[18], as a possible basis for flagging limits to access and disclosure (see 4.2.6.1).

However, this does not imply that data which is not classified as 'sensitive' is unimportant or need not be kept confidential:

- Even information which seems objectively trivial may still be regarded as 'private' – it may not damage your interests if other people know

18 Raymond Wacks proposes a threefold classification of information sensitivity on p227 of *Personal information, privacy and the law*, based on potential for 'serious harm'. He suggests a very detailed classification (p230ff), although not apparently based on evidence of public perceptions. It is broadly congruent with my evidence, but there are differences in detail.

what you had for breakfast or what size shoes you wear, but 'they have no business knowing'.

- Moreover powerful IT makes it possible to accumulate a threateningly rich and detailed picture even from objectively trivial detail in the mass (see 4.2.2.2).

M: 'All personal information should be confidential'

M: 'Who's to say what's trivial to another person?'

(Sth, mid-TEA, 45–64)

4.2.6.1 Assessments of sensitivity

Participants in some sessions were given a list of 18 different types of information, and asked to allot each one a score between 0 and 10 – higher scores mean more important to keep it confidential[19]. Again I have described this as 'sensitivity' of information. The chart overleaf shows the average (mean) scores for each information type, based on ratings made by 38 people.

Remember that *the sample is very small and unsystematic.* Although the broad pattern is interesting, *the specific scores are not shown, since they are not reliable statistical estimates of the wider population.* The ratings could be repeated with a larger sample (and perhaps more categories) if important decisions were to be based on them.

The chart suggests that the most sensitive of the listed topics[20] are:

- information relating to medical tests and health matters (ranks 1st and 5th on average among the 18 factors)
- information about income and savings (ranks 2nd and 4th).

---

19 Some people found this a fairly difficult concept to grasp. Most picked it up after some discussion, and the responses seem reasonably consistent with what they said in the sessions. However three people clearly misunderstood, and their responses were omitted from analysis.

20 The list is not exhaustive, and only types of information likely to be handled by DSS were included. I did not ask about other topics likely to be sensitive – like sexual preferences or voting behaviour, for example.

This ties up with the general drift of the conversations, in which health and finance tended to be talked of as the most sensitive types of information[21].

Perhaps less predictable is the high score for 'partner's circumstances', ranked 3rd. People's comments suggest that there are often real difficulties about providing information about the partner. Contemporary society seems to have moved to a position where even marital partners are often seen as entitled to their own personal privacy, and many feel they 'have no business' giving information about other people, which they argue should be sought direct from the person concerned.

> *F: 'Well what happens then if your partner doesn't want to tell you to put on the form?'*
> *M: 'If my partner wants to divulge information that's up to her'*
>
> (Nth, benefits, 40+)

> *F: 'Every member of the family is an individual and their privacy has the right to be respected, no matter what you thought. You can give out information voluntarily about yourself, but whether you've got a Mum or Dad or siblings, that's up to them to disclose their information, because I've had forms where it says "How many members of your family, name, ages -" and I've refused to put it, because that's not my right to give my family's name and address. If you want to know about me, I'm giving it to you freely, but it's not my right to say "Well, this is my sister's name, this is her address, this is where she –", that's not my right to do that'*
>
> (Lon, lone parent, 16–29)

Sixth in rank in the chart is 'phone number linked to other information'. Phone number and address were listed both 'alone', and 'linked to other information' (eg on a list of people with certain characteristics). In both cases the linked data is (not surprisingly) rated as more sensitive – although as some pointed out, it would then depend on how sensitive the linked information was. Phone number is consistently rated higher than address, whether linked or not – which again fits with the conversation.

---

21 Within these fields there may however be considerable variation – for example some people said they felt that medical information was generally more sensitive than finance, but would rather tell a stranger their blood-group than their bank balance. Indeed some kinds of medical information (like blood group or serious allergies) need to be readily available in case of accident.

Sensitivity of different types of information

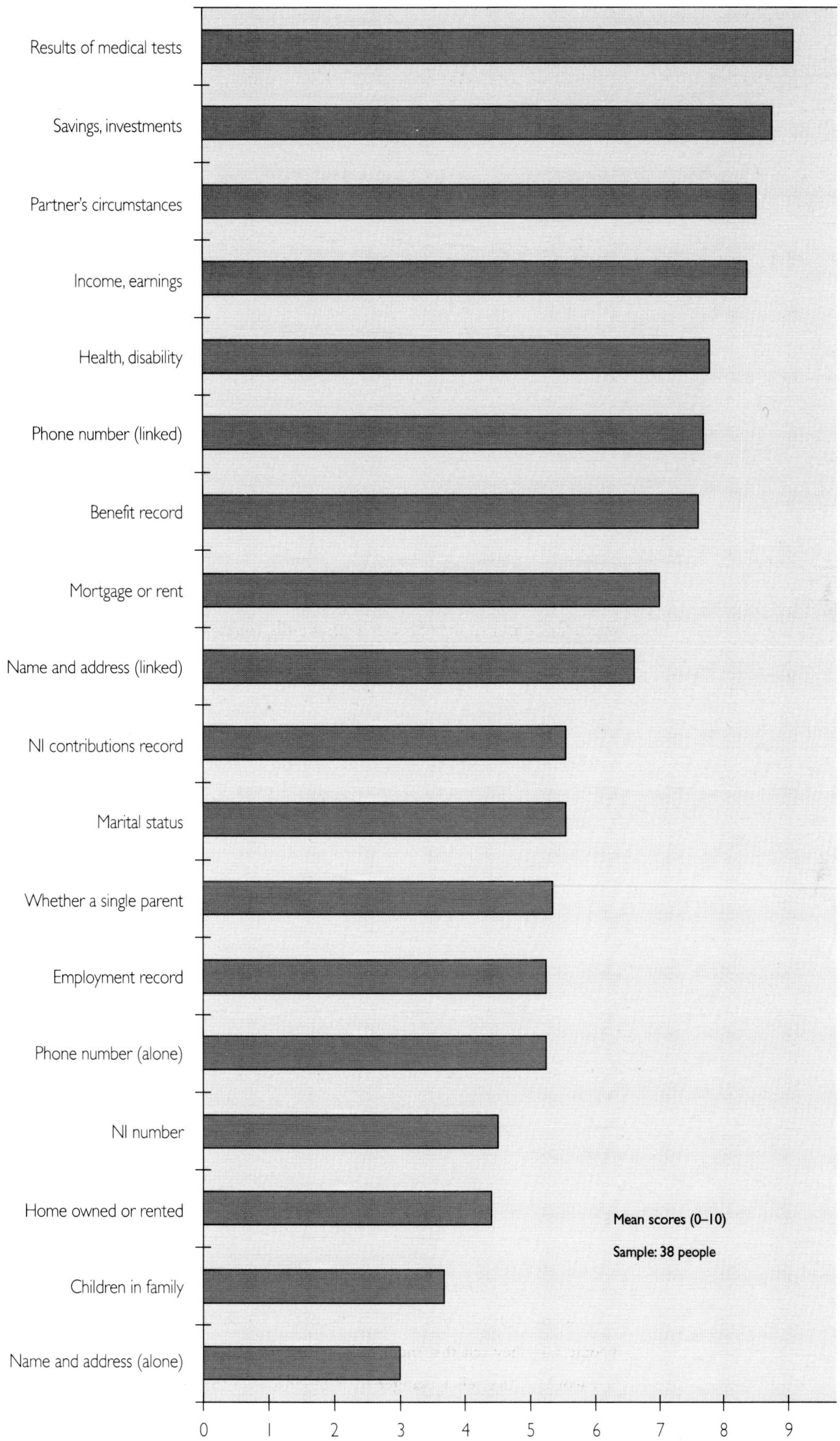

Information	Rank
Phone linked	6th
Address linked	9th
Phone alone	14th
Address alone	18th

'Address alone' is the least sensitive of all the types of information listed – although some people are surprisingly concerned even about that – some don't even like the electoral register being publicly available, since it can be used for compiling junk-mail address lists. Others argue that address alone is public knowledge, and it is only when linked to other information that it becomes important. As we shall see from the scenarios (see 4.3.4.3) address is often seen as very important when it comes to tracing individuals, however. It also becomes extremely important to people who do not want to be traced – for example women separated from violent partners.

People tend to be more concerned about phone number than address, because the phone is seen to be intrusive. There is a surprising level of ex-directory numbers, and although this is sometimes a response to a particular problem (nuisance calls, violent ex-partners and so on), it quite often simply reflects a wish for privacy – limiting and controlling who has telephone access.

'Benefit record' (the benefits people get or have had) is seen to be sensitive (7th rank). This is partly because it is seen to be 'private' information, but also because receipt of benefit is often felt to stereotype, or even stigmatise – recipients may fear that others will look down on them, or be less willing to offer them work, credit etc if information about this leaks out.

The *amount* of mortgage or rent paid ranks 8th, but *whether* they own or rent ranks lower at 16th. Again the financial element is important.

National Insurance (NI) 'contributions record and employment record' (where they have worked and when) are both fairly sensitive (rank 10th and 13th). NI number is slightly less sensitive (15th). Some people see NI number as a fairly public matter, others think it very personal. A few people realise that NI number can be a key to other information, which makes it seem more important.

'Marital status' is perhaps thought surprisingly sensitive – it ranks 11th. This is partly because people are sometimes sensitive about whether they are married or cohabiting – and cohabitation can become an important issue in benefit claims.

'Single parent' status ranks similarly (11th). Some people (notably some single parents) rate this higher, because again it can seem to stigmatise.

M: 'There's some people that's single parents and they're not bothered, there's other people that are single parents and they don't want people to know'
M: 'Well I am a single parent but why should people know that, apart from the people that it actually concerns? Why should other people know it without me letting them know'

(Nth, benefits, 40+)

M: 'It could maybe give someone an impression of you if they're making some assumptions that go along with being a single parent'

(Sth, mid-TEA, 45–64)

The presence, number or ages of 'children in the family' rank fairly low at 17th. Many argued that this is a simple matter which anyone can observe.

It is worth noting that *most* of this information is seen as sensitive – only 4 out of the 18 items listed get mean scores below 5 out of 10, and seven items score above 7 out of 10.

Raymond Wacks (*op cit*) quotes the following table from survey evidence in the Younger Committee report – now out of date (1972), but an interesting comparison with the above. The table shows the percentage of the sample who would and would 'not object to publication' of each of the 13 listed types of information. I have resorted his table into descending order of 'object'. 'Details of sex life' (which I did not cover) comes top of his list, followed by income and medical history – which also feature at the top end of my chart. The Younger data puts income higher than medical history, which I find surprising – although it is possible that this has changed over time – income is perhaps less of a taboo subject than it used to be, although still very sensitive for most people.

Number objecting to publication of various personal details
[Percentages, reading across]

	Object	Not object
Details of sex-life	87	13
Income	78	22
Medical history	51	49
Political views	42	58
Telephone	34	66
Address	33	67
Religious views	28	72
Leisure activities	22	78
(Wife's) maiden name	18	82
Education	17	83
Occupation	12	88
Race	10	90
Nationality	8	92

Total weighted sample = 1,596

More recent quantitative evidence comes from the Data Protection Registrar's annual omnibus survey (*op cit*). Members of the public were given a list of different types of information and asked to indicate their level of concern about organisations keeping this information without their knowledge. Each year is based on about 1,000 interviews.

Proportion saying very or quite concerned:	1992 %	1993 %	1994 %
Your savings	77	75	74
How much you earn	72	70	68
Medical history	61	62	64
Credit ratings	68	65	63
Court judgements	67	67	62
Your visitors	60	59	59
Education and job history	43	40	38
What you buy	39	32	30
Membership of clubs	27	22	25
What papers you read	14	15	14
Your TV viewing	12	12	13
Your age	15	15	13

The table is sorted into descending order on the '94 figures. This again confirms that savings, earnings and medical history top the list – again the two financial categories here come higher than the medical one. There is a large difference between the figures at top and bottom of the table, confirming that different types of information have different inbuilt sensitivities.

This evidence has implications for sharing information between government departments – the great majority of people think that organisations should not have access to information about their income and savings without their knowledge.

4.3 DSS

Having reviewed general issues relating to personal information the final chapter looks more specifically at the DSS context.

4.3.1 General perceptions of DSS

Everybody seems generally aware of DSS, although:

- many people still call it 'DHSS' – or simply 'the Social'
- understanding of its structure and functions is patchy – the image of benefits tends to dominate, and the NI contributions role is usually much less salient in image.

Many people still seem unaware of the agency-based reorganisation – and even claimants often don't know about the Benefits Agency.

I: 'What is the name of the organisation that you are dealing with, what are they called?'
F: 'I just write to the Department of Health and Social Security'
I: 'Do the words "Benefits Agency" mean anything to you?'
F: 'Not really, no'

(Sth, benefits, 45–64)

In spite of the agency split DSS still tends to be seen as one organisation and one set of related functions – although this is perhaps less true for some people when considering the Child Support Agency, which is well known (even notorious). It tends to some extent to have its own identity, not quite so firmly positioned under the DSS umbrella – although most people are at least dimly aware that it is part of DSS. The CSA often seems to be seen as controversial, and sometimes arouses hostility. Some of its use of PI involves contentious disclosures – for example between ex-partners.

F: 'You've got people on Income Support that's probably broken away from a very violent marriage, and the DHSS – well the CSA, they're getting in touch with these violent men and telling them where they bloody live – I mean good God!'
M: 'There's a bloke who works where I work and he's separated from his wife and they've got a ten year old son, and when it was born she left him, didn't want nothing to do with him at all, she went abroad and now she's come back. Ten years later, out of the blue he gets a letter through the post – Child Support Agency – they've got all his details, she's got what he's earning. I don't think that's right'
F: 'She was given that information without his permission'

(Nth, 16–34)

M: 'If you look at the CSA, for example, look at the blunders they've made – it's just incredible. That's a new scheme they set up with modern technology, modern everything, but they can't get it right in 1995. The CSA is a joke'

(Lon, benefits, 16–39)

In some quarters DSS has a very poor image. This is particularly (but not only or always) true among benefit claimants. The dialogue below (from a group of younger inner-city London benefit claimants) illustrates how hostile and suspicious attitudes can sometimes be. Such negative imagery often makes people cynical and mistrustful about the organisation's uses of information.

M: 'I think the government departments – and I don't just mean DSS – I think most government departments will actually come top of the list of inefficient, unwieldy, un-user friendly conglomerates. Actually going to the DSS is the most appalling experience'
M: 'Depressing'
M: 'People should go along and not have to queue and wait and beg and scream and shout, or be in that environment, because not everyone wants to behave like that'

M: 'And people like sometimes behind the counter are not very friendly, and at least you deserve your dignity anyway'
F: 'Well the fact that you're talking to a glass window, you don't talk to a person over a table like this'
M: 'People get very frustrated because they see the DHSS is a totally useless organisation, they see it that it's so inefficient'
F: 'I've been in there and it's just like a human zoo, it's just a nightmare'
M: 'It's appalling'
F: 'And it's the same all over London generally'
F: 'When you're a single parent and they promise you the money's gonna be there and it's not there the next day, and you ring someone else and they say, "I don't know why she promised you that because" – three people tell you three different stories, and then still you've got not a penny in your hand. You can go and sit there all day, get an emergency payment, and when you get there you're so frustrated you do feel like hitting them. And they're just the innocent person that's there and they get all my rage'
F: 'I think we all feel, everybody who ever has to encounter it feels it's such an unwieldy system and such an horrendous experience that you avoid it at all possible costs, so there's no sense in which you would approach that to find out any information about yourself or anybody else willingly'

(Lon, benefits, 16–39)

F: 'I don't have any reason to doubt that if the police wanted information they can get it from DHSS. I have trust in the banks because the banks are strictly not allowed to give out any information about you'

(Lon, lone parent, 16–29)

M: 'To me what the DSS does, it's more like a closed door, because they only tell you what they want you to know'

(Nth, benefits, 65+)

4.3.2 DSS and personal information

In the benefits context concerns about PI are often swamped by more pressing anxieties about:

- getting what you're entitled to – and sometimes getting it paid
- coping generally with the system
- the way DSS agencies are seen to treat you and deal with you.

Any problems like these usually seem much more immediate than what happens to your personal information. It is not that the latter does not matter to benefits customers, but that these other concerns are apt to be very serious and pressing. Indeed people who feel they have broader problems with the system often tend to be *more* suspicious and mistrustful about the way it uses PI.

However, DSS collects and holds a lot of the kinds of information people think most sensitive – about income, savings, benefits, cohabitation and partners, family break-up, employment, and sometimes medical data, for example. Because it is a large and complex organisation it also exemplifies quite a lot of the worries people have about PI.

> *F: 'The DHSS they know everything, they tend to get into everywhere, they get into the housing, they find information out about the banks, like if you put down you've only got so much savings I would assume they would be able to check that. I was surprised they knew so much. They knew where I lived when I was with the dad, even though I hadn't told them I'd moved here, yet they knew – and I always wondered how they knew. They know more than what you think they know'*
>
> (Mid, lone parent, 30–44)

> *M: 'For example, we once had a communication from London didn't we from the DSS? Now I've never dealt with London in all my life'*
> *I: 'Does it make you feel a bit anxious to feel your name was in files in London and in files in Newcastle?'*
> *M: 'Yeah, I think it does really. There's too many people involved at the DSS, any clerk can come up and refer to your – and they might have really nothing to look at it for'*
>
> (Nth, benefits, 60+)

> *M: 'It doesn't matter what legislation happens, what contracts, what laws, what regulations, what safeguards you have to safeguard information. If you go into the DSS and they say: "Look, we swear on our lives that anything you tell us will not leave this room", OK, and you say, "Ooh, OK then" – a month later, someone comes in and says, "Look, I've got five grand in this bag, sort out the information and it's yours". "Oh yeah, fine, OK". You're not gonna stop corruption'*
>
> (Lon, benefits, 16–39)

Most people concede that DSS needs and has a right to collect sensitive PI. However, many benefit customers question the amount and intrusiveness of the data asked for – the forms seem very long, and include 'very personal' information, whose relevance is not always clear[22].

> *F: 'The things that they do ask you especially down at that DHSS is irrelevant'*
> *F: 'Yeah, they really ask you loads'*
> *F: 'They're asking for information on who's sleeping at your house – what is it to do with them?. What's it to do with them though whether you're courting or gay? If I go down and say that I am living on my own, bringing up a child, what right have they got to say, "Well are you sleeping with anybody?". I feel like saying to them, "Well are you?"'*

---

22 It may well be needed for the assessment of their benefits, but since people don't usually understand the details of regulations this is not apparent.

M: 'They do ask some silly questions'
F: 'I told 'em I was gay'
F: 'Some forms that I had to fill in for this disability was 54 pages long – it took me three weeks to do it. It was far too much, they even wanted to know how many times I went to the toilet'

(Nth, 16–34)

M: 'When you fill out your Income Support forms some of the questions you read on them, you can't see how they're relevant, you just think, "Well I'm entitled to some money because I'm not working, and yet I've still gotta supply all this personal information". Everything from are you disabled, are you blind, is your partner working, information about your parents'
M: 'Ethnic origins'
M: 'There is presumably a reason for a lot of it, but it's not discernible when you're filling out these forms'
F: 'I've often found strange questions on things like Housing Benefit forms about whether you live at the front of the house or the back, and you've no idea what kind of picture they're trying to build up, because they seem to have no relation to the kind of way most people live'
M: 'I think it's fair enough if you know the reason why they want this information, but it's not really made clear. Maybe there is something sinister behind it – I wouldn't be surprised'
F: 'And they're like books as well – for someone that's not very good with forms, that's another thing, just seeing the form in front of you. I believe people just don't bother signing on because they can't cope with – they just give up and rather have no money'
M: 'Well that's the way they want it, isn't it – they don't have to pay you benefit if you don't bother filling in the form'
F: 'Yeah, you just think, "Oh, I can't be bothered now, and I wouldn't want everybody to know my past". But part of me thinks, "Who gives a shit?, 'cos who are they?"'

(Lon, benefits, 16–39)

Few people currently feel they can access their DSS records, but this is felt important.

F: 'As long as the individual too can check that – that's another terribly important thing, check that the information they have on their database is correct, very important'

(Sth, graduates, 35–44)

For some people the most visible and aggravating PI issue with DSS is lack of privacy in local BA offices.

F: 'I think if you have ever been in the department and sat there you lose that privacy, by the fact that you have actually been in there, in one of those departments and sat there and had your whole life drawn out of you in front of a glass screen. Well I did feel that there were people as near to me as you are that could have heard everything that I was saying. Not that I was saying anything that I did not really want – but it was personal and at that time I was quite upset. I feel that once they have processed it everybody that works on the other side of the glass window as such is actually working for them and so they need to know that'

(Sth, benefits, 45–64)

F: 'When you fill in for like Housing Benefit and so forth you hand them in, they just go to whoever collects them and they just put 'em in a tray and they are laying there for all and sundry to be able to go looking through, which does hold confidential things about yourself'
M: 'I don't think there's enough security'
F: 'They wander around. They've got no set job. They just go and leaf through papers. They could be highly confidential. And you don't know who they are. You don't know if they're a cleaner or the Manager of the office'
F: 'Anyone in the office could have heard what was happening'
F: 'They should have private rooms where they interview'
F: 'After all it's rather personal isn't it, your personal affairs'
F: 'As far as I'm concerned that wasn't very confidential because I had to speak to nearly everyone several times and everything was passed round the office'

(Lon, pensioners)

4.3.3 Clarifying the DSS status of PI

DSS (like many other bodies) is not felt to explain the status of the information collected. People do not feel they are told what happens to it, who has access, and where it may travel to.

I: 'Do you think information you provide to DSS could ever end up with you getting junk mail, does it get passed on?'
F: 'Yeah, you can buy mailing lists'
M: 'I don't think so. It would be helpful if these things were clarified when you were claiming. When you go to DSS they don't tell you, they don't say, "This information's not gonna be given from this department"'
I: 'Would you believe them if they did?'
M: 'Probably not'
F: 'I think it's important to set up the terms clearly'

(Lon, benefits, 16–39)

The information given seems variable:

a) The Customer Charter: The BA Customer Charter[23] is not helpful about this. Leaflet CUST.1 (1993) only says:

---

23 Very few people seem aware of this in any case.

CONFIDENTIAL What you tell us is protected by the Social Security and Data Protection Acts. If you want a private interview please ask us[24].

I sometimes read this paragraph to participants. Saying information is 'confidential' without explaining what this means is not much help. Some people may feel vaguely reassured, but it does not begin to tell what most want to know. It gives no clues whether or not confidentiality would be breached if PI were disclosed to another office of the same agency; to another DSS agency; to the LA Housing Benefit Office; to the UB office; to the Inland Revenue; to other governments; to the police; to the media; to landlords or employers; to commercial companies; or to other individuals.

The only 'explanation' the Charter gives is by quoting statutes (the DPA and Social Security Acts). This again is no help – even the most relevant provisions of the DPA are not widely known (4.2.4.1), and those I spoke to rarely had the slightest clue what the Social Security Acts might say about confidentiality. People tend to assume that Government Departments normally operate within the law (and certainly that they would claim to do so) – but that is not reassuring or useful if you don't know how well that law protects your interests.

M: 'I mean what is the Act, nobody knows the Act do they?'
I: 'Have you heard of the Data Protection Act?'
M: 'No, well I don't think I've heard of that'
I: 'And the Social Security Acts'
M: 'Not really, no. Nothing at all to me'

(Mid, benefits, 45–64)

b) Other BA documents: There was no time in the sessions to show participants copies of other BA documents to get reactions to what they say about confidentiality. I have not made an exhaustive study of DSS forms and literature from this point of view, but I did look at some examples. Comments about PI and confidentiality seem to vary a lot – some make broad statements, others say little or nothing. For example:

- **Incapacity Benefit Form (SC1 April '95):** Says little. Part 19 (declaration) says that:
  – DSS can ask doctors who have treated the claimant

24 We have seen that privacy at the point of delivering personal information (notably at the counter) is an important preoccupation for some. A number of people said they would have liked a private interview, but were not offered one, or given the impression it would be available.

– the information can be used to assess this or any other benefit claimed.

- **IS claim pack (A1):** The notes have a section headed 'Data Protection Act', which says 'The information you provide will be used to process your claim for IS. Some of the information may be checked with other sources. The information may be used for other purposes relating to the work of the DSS. It will be given to other people only as permitted by law'.

- **FC claim pack FC1 (July 1995):** Does not seem to say anything in notes or forms.

None of these really seem to clarify the situation in the terms people would like. The first two contain fragments, but no real meat. For example in the IS statement: What 'other purposes' might the DSS have? Which 'other people'? What is 'permitted by law'?

It is easy to criticise the present lack of clarification, but the task of satisfying people's needs is in truth difficult, because of the enormous complexity of the web of possible disclosures, bodies involved, types of information, reasons for transfer etc (see 4.1.3.2). If statements are not fairly definite and specific they will not be useful; yet if they are not very brief and simple most people will probably not read or digest them.

And in any case such statements might well be overlooked in crowded and demanding forms and leaflets – people are concerned about the uses of PI but that is not usually their main worry when filling in a claim form or trying to assess eligibility.

> *F: 'We're just so happy to get our money we don't really care where the information goes. All I'm interested in is getting my giro every Monday'*
> (Lon, benefits, 16–39)

4.3.4 Scenarios

Participants were given a series of disclosure scenarios, chosen from a basic set of 40, prepared by DSS in discussion with Alan Hedges (full texts in Annex V). These generally worked well.

4.3.4.1 Presentation of scenarios

The basic approach was to read out a scenario and ask participants to put two ticks on a questionnaire to show:

- whether they thought the disclosure *would* currently be made

- whether it *should* be made in their opinion.

Other scenarios followed, until each session had judged 6 to 12 of them. Scenarios were not systematically rotated – I used mainly those which worked well, proved interesting and/or fitted each conversation. Some were used very little. Scenarios were not presented as standardised texts –

wording was often partly extemporised, and the content was sometimes deliberately varied to explore perceptions. Reactions to the scenarios were discussed briefly – usually only after all the reactions had been recorded, but sometimes (mainly in depth interviews) as they were presented. Finally, participants were usually given an indication of DSS's expressed policy about each scenario they had considered.

Because of the deliberately unsystematic presentation and the small numbers involved the results must not be treated as firm statistical evidence. Again the broad patterns of response are more important than the detail.

A fuller set of scenario results is shown and discussed in 4.3.4.3. The broad pattern of results for the most frequently used scenarios (those judged by 20 people or more) is shown in the chart on the next page. The chart shows net percentages for 'would' and 'should'. These are calculated by subtracting the percentage who say 'would not' from the percentage who say 'would', and similarly for 'should not' and 'should'. The light bars show the 'would' results, and the dark bars the 'should'. The chart is arranged in descending order of 'should'.

4.3.4.2 General reactions to scenarios

Reactions to these scenarios were interesting:

- People often wanted to make finely shaded or qualified judgements in response to them
- Some cases were felt to present tricky moral dilemmas
- Participants often remarked that they were guessing about what present practice would be
- Where people assumed DSS would *not* provide the information requested this was more often ascribed to practical considerations than to ethical scruples – they haven't got the staff, might make trouble for themselves, might get adverse publicity, couldn't be bothered etc.

The pattern of answers suggests the following general conclusions.

a) Presumption of confidentiality: Most people felt there should be an overarching presumption in favour of confidentiality – which should normally only be set aside for very important and compelling reasons (like serious crime or individuals at risk).

b) Children at risk: Participants often found cases like children or young people at risk (Scenarios 10 and 11) difficult to determine – they often sparked off debate. People usually feel that the matters at stake here are easily important enough to override confidentiality, but they often present complex dilemmas quite apart from confidentiality issues – for

Would and should be done: net percentages

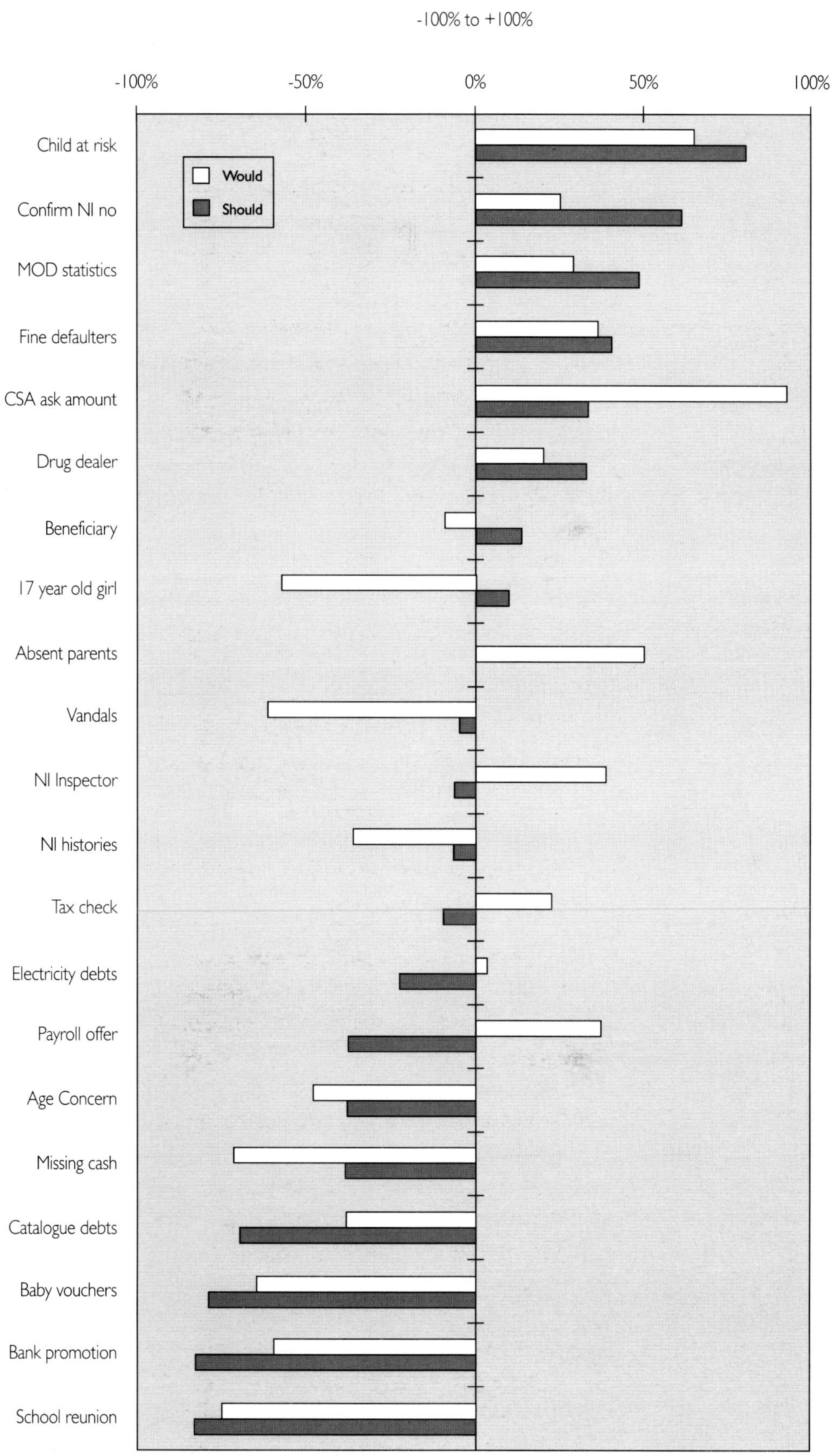

example whether a runaway child may be more or less at risk if sent home. Some argued that DSS may not have the competence or the information to resolve such dilemmas – in which case perhaps it should be releasing the information to competent authorities like Social Services or the police rather than to the parents.

c) 'Good causes': Helping 'good causes' is not generally seen to justify over-riding confidentiality, unless there is a very serious need.

d) Cross-checking: Cross-checking between government databases to prevent or detect fraud is controversial – views divide, some people are ambivalent. But most feel that any checking should be limited in scale and based on reasonable grounds for suspicion in particular cases. Information should not be routinely shared between government departments.

e) Commercial purposes: There was almost universal agreement that DSS should not under any circumstances release PI for commercial purposes.

f) Debtors: The general view was that DSS should not provide the addresses of debtors, unless requested on proper authority by the courts or police – and 'proper authority' here probably means through legal process.

g) Landlords: Most people felt that DSS should not provide information about tenants direct to landlords – certainly not without the tenant's consent. Landlords should get information from their tenants, not from DSS. DSS may provide tenants at their request with written information which they can give to the landlord.

h) Employers: As with landlords most people felt that information about employees should not normally be supplied direct to employers – apart perhaps from purely administrative details necessary for operating NI deductions. Again written information could be supplied to employees to pass on to employers at their discretion.

i) Statistics: Releasing information in purely statistical form is usually thought to be in order – confidentiality issues don't arise if there is no way individuals can be identified.

4.3.4.3 Scenarios in detail

Annex V lists all 40 scenarios in full with summaries of current DSS policies. The boxes below show:

- summarised texts of the 28 scenarios which were exposed to 9 people or more
- the number of people considering each (top right)
- the percentages of those people who said the disclosure:
  – would or wouldn't be made (bottom left)

– and should or shouldn't be made (bottom right).

Percentages usually add to less to 100%, because undecided participants are omitted.

Percentages are shown to make comparison easier, but *these are based on very small figures, and must be interpreted broadly and with great caution – they cannot be taken as reliable population estimates*, particularly for judgements based on less than 20–30 cases. Scenarios based on less than 9 judgements have been omitted.

Below each box is a brief comment about the way they were interpreted, and about reactions to declared policy (in bold).

Charities and voluntary bodies

Scenario 6 Only 23 judgements

* A school trying to arrange a reunion asks the DSS to help trace former pupils

Would 4% Wouldn't 78% Should 4% Shouldn't 87%

Not a valid reason for over-riding confidentiality – a purely social purpose. Accept this and you'd have to accept almost anything. **DSS policy of not providing was endorsed.**

Scenario 8 59 judgements

* Age Concern asks DSS for the names and addresses of all pensioners in a particular area, in order to start a pensioners' support group

Would 20% Wouldn't 68% Should 29% Shouldn't 66%

This seems a good cause which might benefit the individuals, and Age Concern is well-known and reputable – these factors swung some votes, but a large majority were still opposed. The information is confidential, there is no powerful reason for over-riding this – and some pensioners might not want to be contacted. **DSS policy of not providing but suggesting alternative routes was endorsed**.

Scenario 31 | Only 10 judgements

★ A CAB advice worker telephones the DSS and asks to discuss Mr X's claim to benefit

Would 60% Wouldn't 30% Should 50% Shouldn't 50%

This was not often asked about. Opinion seemed divided. The general view seems to be that advice agencies should have no rights of access without their client's permission, but DSS should co-operate fully if the worker has authenticated authority. **DSS policy (co-operating in bona fide cases with subject consent) is usually endorsed – but not just on the basis of a phone call.**

Private sector companies

Scenario 1 | 67 judgements

★ A baby food company asks the DSS Child Benefit Centre for the names and addresses of all new mothers, so it can send complimentary baby care vouchers (worth £25)

Would 12% Wouldn't 76% Should 9% Shouldn't 88%

Overwhelming opinion against providing these. Most think DSS shouldn't give information for commercial purposes. A minority argued that the mothers would gain from it – but there are seen to be other established ways of delivering such offers, and some suspect commercial follow-up pressure – 'you'd never have them off your back'. **DSS policy of non-cooperation generally endorsed.**

Scenario 4 | 45 judgements

★ A direct mail catalogue company asks DSS to help trace people who have moved without paying their outstanding debts

Would 22% Wouldn't 60% Should 9% Shouldn't 78%

Again very strong opposition. This is nothing to do with DSS, the information is confidential, and this is a commercial organisation which has other ways of tracing debtors. **DSS policy (non-cooperation without court order) widely endorsed.**

Scenario 5 34 judgements

* A bank wanting to attract new young customers asks DSS for the names and addresses of everybody allocated a National Insurance number

Would 15% Wouldn't 74% Should 9% Shouldn't 91%

Overwhelming opposition to a purely commercial scheme with no benefit to the individuals concerned. **DSS policy of non-cooperation generally endorsed**.

Scenario 15 Only 9 judgements

* A life assurance company asks DSS for the names and addresses of people receiving a terminally ill benefit so that they can offer their services

Would 11% Wouldn't 78% Should 11% Shouldn't 89%

Only exposed to 9 people, who were very strongly opposed – consistent with other commercial cases. **DSS policy of non-disclosure probably widely approved**.

Scenario 19 68 judgements

* An Electricity Company asks DSS to help locate an occupier who has left with a large unpaid bill

Would 41% Wouldn't 38% Should 31% Shouldn't 53%

Majority opposed, but considerably more support than with catalogue company debts (Scenario 4) – mainly because electricity (even post-privatisation[25]) has a more 'public service' image, seen as a basic necessity, 'You can't live without electricity, you can live without catalogues'. This is also why 2 in 5 thought DSS *would* provide this information. **DSS policy (non-cooperation) widely supported – but evoked some surprise**.

25 Although interestingly a few people changed their minds when they remembered that electricity supply has entered the private sector, and decided the information should not now be provided.

Employers

Scenario 36 — 34 judgements

* A security company asks DSS for the National Insurance contribution histories of employees to comply with a British Standard requirement for 10 year employment records

Would 29% Wouldn't 65% Should 41% Shouldn't 47%

Fairly even division of opinion. Some favoured verification rather than disclosure. Some wanted employee's consent. This is a commercial company, but not just a commercial application – people understand that this kind of information is needed. Yet the information should be confidential in principle. **DSS policy satisfied most people – giving it to the employee on request, not to the employer.**

Scenario 37 — 23 judgements

* Several large companies ask DSS for a service whereby they can telephone and confirm the NI number an employee has provided

Would 61% Wouldn't 35% Should 78% Shouldn't 17%

Large majority in favour – and most assume DSS would do it. Confirmation of NI number does not seem threatening – and it is information the employer must have. Some were unhappy about responding to telephone enquiries. **The research briefing was that DSS would only give this information to employees, not to employers. This seemed more restrictive than most participants expected or asked for – but people generally seemed happy with it as a sensible compromise. DSS later said that the original statement was wrong, in that NI numbers could be *verified* to employers who already have them. This notion was not tried out specifically, although I found in other points of the discussion that verification is likely to be more acceptable than straight disclosure.**

Scenario 25 — 24 judgements

* An employer asks if DSS can help trace an employee who disappeared when a large amount of cash went missing

Would 4% Wouldn't 75% Should 29% Shouldn't 67%

Clear majority opposed – this is not DSS's business, it should be pursued by the police, the person might be innocent. On the other hand some argued it is important to detect the crime. **DSS policy of non-disclosure on mere suspicion was widely endorsed**.

Scenario 26 — 27 judgements

* A large company has offered DSS access to payroll records so that it can check if any employees are working whilst claiming benefit. Should DSS accept?

Would 63% Wouldn't 26% Should 26% Shouldn't 63%

The majority assume that DSS would not be able to resist the offer – but thought they should refuse it. This seems 'Big Brotherish' to many. A largish minority advocated acceptance because they disapprove of fraudulent claims. **DSS policy of not accepting was widely endorsed – but sometimes greeted with scepticism**.

M: 'I think they would'
F: 'Yeah, it's a chance to catch people out'
M: 'They say they wouldn't, but they would'
M: 'They love to catch up without you knowing'

(Lon, benefits, 16–39)

DSS internal

Scenario 28 — 51 judgements

* A National Insurance Inspector is satisfied with a routine inspection of a local firm but takes a precautionary copy of the company's payroll and passes it to a colleague in the Benefits Agency

Would 65% Wouldn't 25% Should 41% Shouldn't 47%

The majority again felt that DSS would do this, but opinion was divided about whether they should. On the one hand detecting fraud seems desirable – 'If you're stupid enough to claim the stuff and then go and work you're asking for it'. On the other hand this seems to infringe the individual's rights, and again smacks of Big Brother – 'a lot of people'd be checked up on who've done nothing wrong'. **DSS policy of requiring reasonable grounds for suspicion and rejecting 'fishing expeditions' seemed the right balance – although some see DSS as perennially suspicious and fear this policy could justify anything**.

Scenario 29 — 32 judgements

* The Benefits Agency asks the Child Support Agency to provide details of any absent parent with a new partner. The BA want the CSA to provide a list detailing both the absent parent's and the new partner's name, address, and NI no.

Would 66% Wouldn't 16% Should 44% Shouldn't 44%

Again most people assume DSS would do this, but opinion is divided about what should happen, for reasons similar to Scenario 28. Most people think information can be exchanged fairly freely within DSS, but the CSA does have a more separate and controversial image. **DSS policy (again reasonable suspicion not general trawling) strikes most as a good (if not always credible) compromise**.

Scenario 34 — 36 judgements

* Child Support Agency ask Benefits Agency for the amount of benefit paid to an absent parent receiving Incapacity Benefit

Would 94% Wouldn't 3% Should 61% Shouldn't 28%

Almost everyone thinks DSS would do this, and a majority (about 2:1) agree they should. Again most feel that DSS agencies can be allowed to share fairly freely (see 4.3.5.1). Opposition again tends to stem from dislike or mistrust of the CSA – 'From what I've been hearing in the media, and the trouble they've caused'. **DSS policy quotes the legislation – which doesn't generally mean much or cut much ice – but the policy of disclosure is fairly widely supported**.

Government Departments

Scenario 12 — 42 judgements

* The Lord Chancellor's Department asks DSS to help trace fine defaulters

Would 60% Wouldn't 24% Should 67% Shouldn't 26%

Most participants thought DSS would co-operate, and thought they should (majorities over 2:1). Many assumed this would have the backing of the courts – tantamount to a court order, and possibly leaving DSS no option. **DSS policy (non-cooperation) surprised many**.

Scenario 21 — 67 judgements

* DSS asks Inland Revenue for up-to-date information on all tax-payers to confirm that tax declarations are consistent with information on benefit claims

Would 52% Wouldn't 30% Should 39% Shouldn't 48%

A small majority thought this shouldn't happen (although they guessed it would). However quite a lot of people took the opposite view. Again the desire to preserve confidentiality and avoid Big Brother often wrestled with a conflicting desire to track down fraud. **People generally approved (but often didn't believe) the stated Inland Revenue policy of preserving confidentiality**.

Scenario 24 — Only 9 judgements

* The Ministry of Defence want to provide the DSS with a list of service personnel who have gone AWOL. Should DSS accept this list, and should they give the military the latest address of anyone on the list who makes a claim for benefit?

Would 33% Wouldn't 33% Should 11% Shouldn't 56%

Only 9 people considered this case. They were divided about whether DSS would, but tended to think it should not happen. **DSS policy would be to consider the seriousness of the offences.**

Scenario 30 — Only 15 judgements

* The Family Credit unit are concerned that some earnings declarations may be incorrect, and they ask the Inland Revenue to check

Would 73% Wouldn't 7% Should 67% Shouldn't 20%

Only 15 people consider this scenario. Most thought it would happen, and the majority seemed content with this. **DSS policy (to ask for wage slips) seemed agreed (although not always believed) – but the evidence is limited**.

Individuals

Scenario 7 — Only 9 judgements

* Mr X asks DSS to help trace Mr Y who has failed to pay compensation ordered by the court

Would 0% Wouldn't 89% Should 11% Shouldn't 78%

Only 9 people considered this scenario. They thought strongly that DSS would not and should not agree. **DSS non-disclosure policy was approved by the few who heard it**.

Scenario 39 — 47 judgements

* A solicitor cannot locate a major beneficiary under a will, and asks DSS to provide an address

Would 30% Wouldn't 38% Should 51% Shouldn't 38%

Opinions were again divided, but on balance the view was that DSS should co-operate – but probably wouldn't. The argument in favour was that the news sounds welcome – although a few pointed out there might be some catch. **DSS policy of offering a letter-forwarding service was usually seen as an imaginative and satisfactory approach**.

Young people

Scenario 10			67 judgements
* The parents of a 17 year old girl who has run away from her home in the North of England ask the DSS for the address of their daughter who they believe has settled in the King's Cross area of London			
Would 12%	Wouldn't 70%	Should 49%	Shouldn't 40%

This scenario triggered much discussion. Most people thought DSS wouldn't co-operate, but opinions divided about whether they should. The discussion did not hinge round whether the situation was important enough to over-ride confidentiality – most agreed that it clearly was, and a lot of concern was expressed. The argument was about:

- whether the girl is (legally or morally) of an age to make her own decision; and
- why she left, and whether she is necessarily going to be better off at home than in King's Cross – the possibility of abuse etc.

M: 'I think they should. I don't know if they do but I would like to think they do because I'm just imagining if it was my son or daughter'
I: 'How would you react if it was known that the girl had specifically requested that her parents shouldn't know where she was?'
M: 'As long as she's not a minor then she should be entitled to – '
I: 'Well she's 17 in this case'
M: 'It's a bit difficult with the ages, where do you draw the line? I think they should respect her wishes if she's of an age'
F: 'There are other agencies for finding lost children'

(Sth, benefits, 30–44)

M: 'Well if the girl run away and she doesn't want her parents to know, and she told the DSS, "I don't want no-one to know where I live", well they shouldn't, no – because you never know what happened to the family, she could be sexually assaulted by her dad or her mum'

(Lon, benefits, 16–29)

F: 'See I work with a lot of kids that have been abused by parents, and I honestly think that a lot of those people would hate the thought of their parents trying to find where they are half the time'
M: 'Yeah but if they're minors they're just as much likely to be abused in Kings Cross'

(Sth, graduates, 35–44)

These are seen to be complex issues which DSS is not well placed to resolve. Again some argued for passing the case to Social Services or the police – although it is an important case it is not really seen as DSS's business. **DSS policy is not to co-operate – some would favour taking some action, but probably not simply telling the parents**.

Scenario 32 — 67 judgements

* A social worker dealing with a case of a child at risk whose parents have separated and asks DSS to provide the father's address

Would 73% Wouldn't 9% Should 87% Shouldn't 7%

The general view was that DSS would and should co-operate – a child at risk is much more important than maintaining confidentiality of addresses, and the involvement of a social worker probably implies that disclosure is in the child's interest – although some queried this assumption. **DSS policy of co-operating with serious need was generally approved**.

Landlords

Scenario 3 — 50 judgements

* A group of young lads have left their former address owing rent arrears and having vandalised the property. The landlord asks DSS for their whereabouts[26]

Would 14% Wouldn't 74% Should 38% Shouldn't 42%

Opinion divided about whether DSS should provide the address – but most thought they would not. Many people were torn between on the one hand disapproval of the vandalism and a desire to see the perpetrators caught, and on the other hand the general view that this is a private matter which DSS has no part in. **DSS policy of providing information only with a court order won general approval**.

> *M: 'Two ways of answering that. I don't think they should, regards giving information out, but I'd like to see someone get them. They should be caught, put it that way'*
>
> (Mid, benefits, 45–64)

---

26 The full scenario added an element of indemnification by the landlord, but this seemed too complex, and was left out of the scenario as presented.

M: 'Much as my sympathy's with the landlord it's a question of individuals again'
M: 'Well it's criminal damage'
M: 'Yes but it's at the wrong level. It's the police who should be investigating. Maybe they should give information that way, but not to the landlord'

(Lon, pensioners)

Media

Scenario 17 — Only 9 judgements

* The DSS is criticised in the Press for paying benefit to what is popularly viewed as an undeserving case. The claimant has admitted getting benefit and given DSS permission to discuss the case with a reporter – should DSS reveal new facts?

Would 11% Wouldn't 67% Should 44% Shouldn't 44%

Only 9 people considered this scenario. Opinions were divided about what should happen, but most assumed DSS would not co-operate. **DSS policy is not to disclose**.

Police

Scenario 22 — 53 judgements

* A police sergeant investigating a drug trafficking offence asks a local DSS office for the address of someone he needs to speak to

Would 49% Wouldn't 28% Should 60% Shouldn't 28%

Opinions divided about 2:1 in favour of providing this information. Support was largely motivated by the feeling that drug dealing is a serious and repugnant crime. The reservations arose mainly because it is not clear why the police want to speak to the person, and sometimes because disclosure was felt to need higher than sergeant-level authorisation. While they want action on serious crime, many people do not totally trust the police, and certainly feel that personal information should not go to the police except for important reasons and subject to clear controls.

Scenario 23 was never offered for separate rating, but was sometimes introduced as a modification to Scenario 22. In this case a police inspector asks DSS for the address of someone charged with shoplifting. Most seem to agree that drug-dealing is important enough to over-ride confidentiality of address, but shop-lifting is not. **DSS policy (co-operating for serious crimes) was usually approved**.

Research

Scenario 35	35 judgements
* The Ministry of Defence wants to monitor unemployment levels among ex-service personnel, and want DSS to provide statistics only for supplied blocks of National Insurance numbers representing various categories of servicemen	
Would 60% Wouldn't 31%	Should 74% Shouldn't 26%

Most people feel that this is in order providing only statistics are given, and individuals cannot be identified. **DSS policy (providing anonymised information) is widely endorsed**.

Scenario 16	Only 9 judgements
* A researcher writes asking DSS to provide him with the names and addresses of any surviving first world war veterans, so he can interview them and record their memories for posterity (profits to charity)	
Would 44% Wouldn't 56%	Should 56% Shouldn't 44%

Only 9 people considered this. Opinions divided. **DSS policy is not to disclose**.

4.3.5 Sharing DSS data with other bodies

Many people are very hazy about the structure, functions and relationships of government and other organisations in society – yet without some grip on this it is hard to grapple with the full ramifications of data disclosure. I therefore showed a very simplified[27] diagram of some of the main possible players (see next page) to help them express ideas about how DSS should relate to various other kinds of body. This seemed helpful, and participants were often able to make quite sharp distinctions in discussing the kinds of information relationship they felt DSS should have with different kinds of

27 I explained that DSS is actually a part of central government, not separate from it; that some DSS agencies (like War Pensions) are omitted; that most of the key functions of government and local government are not shown; and so on.

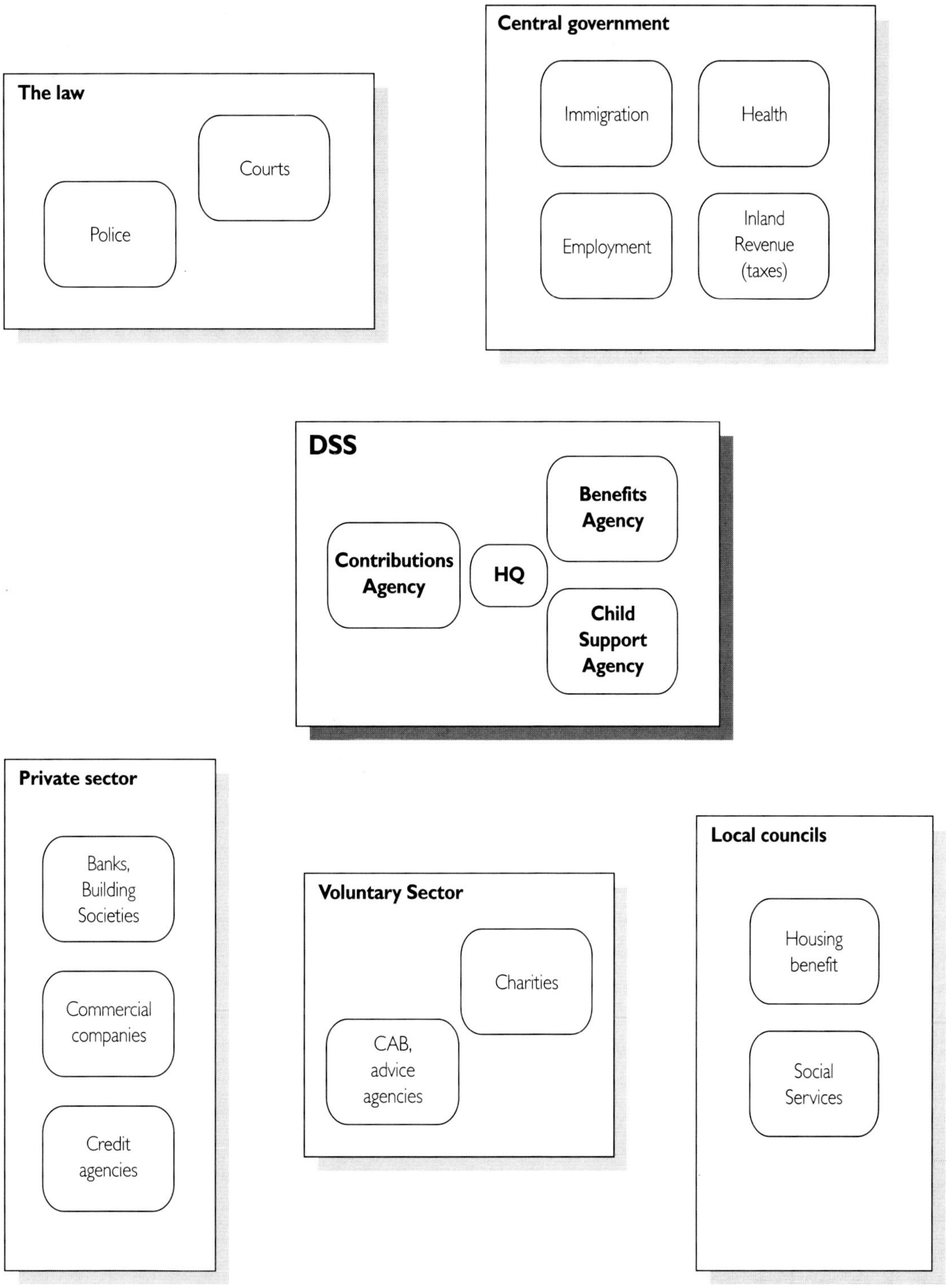
The law
Courts
Police
Central government
Immigration
Health
Employment
Inland Revenue (taxes)
DSS
Benefits Agency
Contributions Agency
HQ
Child Support Agency
Private sector
Banks, Building Societies
Commercial companies
Credit agencies
Voluntary Sector
Charities
CAB, advice agencies
Local councils
Housing benefit
Social Services

body. The main impressions about data relationships which came from this (and from the scenarios and other material) are summarised below.

4.3.5.1 Internal sharing

Most people tend to think it is in order for DSS to share information fairly freely between its component agencies. These are still often thought of as one organisation (4.3.1), and largely seen as having common purposes. The general going-in position is therefore that information within the Department can usually be shared and possibly pooled. This view tended to be taken (perhaps surprisingly) by benefit claimants as well as others. Some hope that it would lead to better service.

> *I: 'So you would be quite happy if there was just a DSS file on you which the various benefits and sections and agencies used?'*
> *F: 'I thought that's what they did'*
> *I: 'So that would not worry you at all?'*
> *F: 'No'*
> *I: 'You don't feel that that is getting to a "Big Brotherish" situation?'*
> *F: 'No, because at the moment if you apply for something you have to apply to one place and they send you to another place, and then you have to go through all the palaver again'*
>
> (Sth, benefits, 45–64)

> *M: 'I think that if they didn't work as one they'd be the most inefficient organisation in the world'*
> *M: 'I don't see how they can work unless they do'*
> *F: 'They're like one company – DSS is one company'*
> *M: 'If you look, Benefits and Contributions Agency have to be together, 'cause the Benefits Agencies pays for the Contributions Agency. And the Child Support Agency takes money off Income Support for Child Benefit and such like, so they have to work together, it'd be impossible not to'*
>
> (Lon, benefits, 16–39)

> *M: 'They should exchange because it used to be one department – and it were probably better when it were one department because they only had one set of gaffers and now you've got – '*
> *M: 'More chiefs than Indians'*
> *F: 'You ring up and "Oh your book's somewhere else, oh it's somewhere else", you've got to keep ringing up and being put through to different departments'*
>
> (Nth, benefits, 40+)

Sometimes this view broke down a little when looking more closely at the details – particularly in relation to the CSA. As a new body this was never part of the pre-agency DSS monolith, and it has a more separate identity in some minds. It is also sometimes seen as rather different in objectives. CSA has a more controversial image, and poses in detail some difficult PI issues (like potential disclosure of a new partner's circumstances to a previous partner, and vice versa). Some were therefore less happy about free sharing if this included CSA – it was interesting that the only group which did not largely see DSS as one single information unit was one which had already been complaining vociferously about the CSA.

Nevertheless some would be quite happy to see fairly complete pooling of information within DSS, while others would prefer selective controls:

- access on a need-to-know basis only
- access to some information needing justification or special permission
- access limited by classification of staff and/or type of information.

M: 'I certainly would support that staff would have to follow a particular route – you'd have the initial input to say yes that can happen, and that route would be sufficiently stiff that would make them think, "Is this information really necessary cos I've gotta go down a particular road to get it, it's gonna be quite hard". I don't have a problem with that but I wouldn't agree with free-flow information'
(Sth, graduates, 35–44)

M: 'It could be a common computer but they'd have to ask'
F: 'They shouldn't be able to tap into it just like that'
(Mid, low-TEA, 45–64)

4.3.5.2 Sharing with other government departments

It is widely assumed that government departments do already share or exchange information fairly extensively and freely – the image probably outstrips the reality.

M: 'All other government departments throughout the UK can interlink, it's obvious – and if they can't interlink there's telephones, and there's ways and means'
(Mid, low-TEA, 45–64)

I: 'So you're saying the police can find out what's on your benefit form or what's on your passport form?'
F: 'Oh yeah, yeah, yeah'
F: 'Of course they can, yeah'
I: 'Just without necessarily getting a court order or something like that?'
F: 'All they have to do is print your name into the computer and up it comes doesn't it, everything'
F: 'They probably have to get a court order to use that information against you, but yes, they can get hold of that information'
F: 'I'm on the unemployment benefit at the moment, as soon as I signed on to that the Tax Office wrote to me to say, "What have you been doing in x amount of months?", so to me they must have immediately informed each other because they rang exactly on the same lines of what I'd just informed the Benefit Office about'
(Nth, 16–34)

M: 'The police, the Social Security and the Inland Revenue's computers are linked aren't they? I believe they are – or they're certainly in the process of linking those three'
(Mid, graduates, 35–44)

M: 'I imagine they share anything that they're asked to provide basically, I shouldn't think there's any confidentiality at all'
I: 'So if you put something on your tax form that would be known to the Department of Social Security if they want to find out?'
M: 'Any government department could probably lay their hands on it quite easily'
F: 'I think I'd probably assume that they could, but that there were probably guidelines saying they shouldn't'

(Sth, graduates, 35–44)

I: 'Do you think that the Department of Social Security would ring up the Tax office and say, "We want information about what people put in their tax forms so we can cross-check them for benefits". Do you think that happens?'
F: 'Of course'
F: 'Yes'
M: 'I don't think they do it officially, but I'd be surprised if it didn't happen'
F: 'I don't think it's supposed to happen'

(Lon, benefits, 16–39)

Some assume there is already a large centralised government database on individuals – and if there isn't it is probably limited by practical problems (too much information) rather than by policy. Most people assume that things are at least heading in that general direction, if they haven't already arrived there. Any practical difficulties will be overcome by more powerful computers, or by networking.

A minority of participants favoured more extensive sharing of information between Departments – notably between DSS, Inland Revenue and perhaps Employment, mainly to cut down fraud. Indeed a few saw this as a neglected duty.

M: 'If you're giving information to one department and you give different information to another department they're entitled to catch you'

(Mid, benefits, 45–64)

F: 'If it's actually going to stop the fraud, particularly in the DHSS – we all hear about the problems that they're having, the amount of money that's being lost to fraudulent claims, if that's going to stop and the money's going to go back into the pockets of the people that need it, then so be it'

(Mid, graduates, 35–44)

F: 'I think that the government departments should share information, like the DSS should share it with Education to try and prevent all the fraudulent activities'
F: 'That would mean an enormous number of people would have your information. I mean really a vast number'

(Sth, graduates, 35–44)

Most would accept (even welcome) sharing of relevant information connected with a specific functional relationship – for example the Employment Service and BA may need to exchange information about unemployed people – this is not only necessary for benefit and NI administration, but it would also probably help to make life more efficient for customers, who are apt to complain if different agencies involved in a transaction don't pass relevant information between them. People would not complain about this sort of transaction-related transfer, and indeed would often welcome it – *provided* that:

- they are told it will happen
- the information passed is narrow and specific to those transactions, not a broader pooling of data
- it is controlled so that sensitive information is not disclosed without important and relevant reasons
- it is not then passed on to yet further agencies.

F: 'I'd be stressed enough to actually have to go to two different departments to fill out forms. If I'm not au fait with forms they're very daunting, so if I have to actually give all my information to one department but they're now going to send me to the housing, and I go there and they say "Yes Miss so and so, we have everything on the screen, can we just check to see if it's all right", I'm going to feel more relaxed, and I'm going to feel that this department is helping me'

(Mid, graduates, 35–44)

F: 'My father died this year and my mum was put into a very awkward situation, basically she had nothing, and it helped me that having helped fill in one set of forms for her to have Income Support they were gonna help her with the cost of her house as well, that was a completely different building, way across the other side of town, but I didn't have to go through it all again because they were able to communicate with these people, a lot of information was already there. My mother was in a dreadful state at the time anyway, and for me that was just absolutely wonderful, they just took it out of my hands and sorted her out'

(Sth, graduates, 35–44)

Most people would not be happy about a significant increase in government sharing of information, and some suspect or fear it has already gone further than they would like. They would rather it should be:

- kept to a reasonable minimum
- accomplished by selective sharing rather than complete pooling
- and subject to controls and limitations.

M: 'DHSS should not be able to give that information to Inland Revenue, police or whatever until they've contacted me, police have asked me for this, or

Inland Revenue's asked me for this, can I give them the extra number, it should be up to me then to say yes or no'

(Nth, benefits, 40+)

M: 'I think if you could be sure that you could get access to the information and put it right if the information was wrong then I don't really see any problem, but it's being sure that you could get access to that information'
M: 'I'm also concerned as to why information is needed by certain departments. If they want information about my salary, then if it's the Inland Revenue you start to think, "Well that's fine, that's the kind of information they do want", but if the police want information about my salary then I might want to question why they should have that information – or other departments'

(Mid, graduates, 35–44)

The public view tends to be that it is *not* in order to:

- transfer data en masse so that other departments can see if there might be anything of interest; or
- engage in 'fishing expeditions' where there are no grounds for suspecting dishonesty.

I: 'So in other words before DSS could get access to Inland Revenue data they ought to get a court order?'
M: 'Yes'
F: 'I think it's a bit too strong really'
M: 'It depends for what purpose they want the information'
F: 'Don't know about legal, but certainly special permission – not say, "Here you are, here's all the information you want, have it"'

(Mid, low-TEA, 45–64)

M: 'I think maybe either "Needs special permission", or "Available on request for a good reason" – maybe I think more "Need special permission", there's a set of rules or something that have to be followed'
M: 'I think that those procedures should be legally binding'
I: 'And under what circumstances do you think DSS ought to be able to ask the Inland Revenue what somebody's put on their tax form or vice versa?'
F: 'When they're checking out fraud. I can't think of anything else'

(Mid, graduates, 35–44)

The idea of a giant pooled government PI database is not widely accepted, even by most of those who would want tougher anti-fraud action, for reasons given in 4.2.2.2 above:

- it smacks of 'Big Brother'
- 'they'd know too much' about you
- it gives the State too much power
- errors could be disastrous.

F: 'I think I'd probably in the end be against sharing information. You never know if there was going to be a government like the Reich or something who'd want to find out whether you had Jewish parents and if every single department knew – or whether you had blue eyes or whatever it was they decided they were going to – . Equally I feel cynical to think that however many rules you make those are never going to be kept, and everybody who wants to get to know, is always going to be able to get to know'

(Sth, graduates, 35–44)

I: 'If there was a big computer file somewhere which has all the information government knows about you as an individual?'
F: 'No, I wouldn't be happy about it'
M: 'It'd be a bad thing – there's such a thing as a right to privacy'
M: 'I think you're allowed to live your life in a reasonable manner without interference from outside agencies'
M: 'Deserve like a dignity, privacy'
M: 'If somebody does something wrong they pay the – that's a different matter. But if people live a normalish type of existence, then I don't see any reason why somebody somewhere should have information on you'

(Lon, benefits, 16–39)

F: 'I don't think I'd welcome it (centralised database), I don't think I'd want any government to have that amount of power over me'

(Sth, graduates, 35–44)

M: 'I think there can be the Big Brother factor a bit too much, and I think there should be some element of freedom, and I think you'd lose every bit of freedom if it was all tied up like that – you'd be afraid to go out of the blinking house in the morning. It gives so much power to these individuals who work in these departments. If they were of a mind to have a vendetta they could look up everything to do with you. I think you could end up in trouble and you'd have a bit of a job to prove otherwise'

(Sth, benefits, 30–44)

F: 'As long as you know you've been honest and told them the truth it doesn't matter to that extent – because I feel anything they ask you is usually to your own benefit in the end. So unless you've lied then you should not really be worried about who knows about it'
I: 'It would be technically possible for the government to construct some sort of central database in which all the information all the departments have about given individuals was put together'
F: 'No, I don't like that idea'
I: 'What worries you about that?'
F: 'Because that way you might not know who was actually delving into your records. Not unless they had some method of asking you before they accessed it, which would probably cause more problems'

(Sth, benefits, 45–64)

4.3.5.3 Sharing with local authorities (LAs)

Most people feel that government departments should not exchange data with LAs, unless there is a specific transactional relationship. This is the case for example with the administration of Housing Benefit, where BA and the HB authority need to work together – in the customer's interest as well as for efficiency reasons. As with the Employment Service, most people would accept or even welcome transaction-based sharing between these bodies – again provided it is explained to them, controlled, and limited to relevant and essential items.

The impression is that DSS information should not normally be exchanged with Social Services, except with the express permission of the individual, or in cases of exceptional need (eg children at risk). This should require either subject consent or high-level authorisation.

4.3.5.4 Sharing with the police and courts

Most people were very chary about DSS information being divulged to the police or the legal system:

- the police no longer enjoy untrammelled public confidence
- the attention of the police is potentially threatening and unwelcome to individuals – even if they are law-abiding.

Most people feel that PI information should normally only be disclosed to the police:

- with due process – court orders, warrants, high level authorisation etc
- in relation to offences serious enough to warrant violating confidentiality
- not just on vague suspicion
- and certainly not on an indiscriminate trawl.

> *M: 'I don't really think, as pro-police as I am, I don't really think that a lot of this information should be made aware to the police and Inland Revenue'*
> *I: 'How far do you think they should be able to get information from DSS about individuals?'*
> *F: 'I don't think they should'*
> *M: 'None at all'*
> *I: 'Suppose it was somebody who was just suspected of a criminal activity?'*
> *M: 'No'*
> *F: 'No, not when they're just suspected, no it needs to be proven first'*
> *M: 'Well it's like going into a person's home and you need a court order, they should be the same. You should have a court order to get information'*
> (Mid, low-TEA, 45–64)

Some more flexibility may be needed for serious crime.

4.3.5.5 Sharing with the private sector: Most people were adamant that they want strong bi-directional firewalls between DSS and the private sector[28].

Participants could think of virtually no circumstances which would justify DSS giving PI to commercial organisations.

- There would be very strong disapproval if DSS supplied mailing lists or names and addresses for marketing or publicity purposes
- PI should not normally be disclosed to landlords or employers – although:
  - if necessary tenants and employees could be given certificates to show.
  - it would probably be in order to verify necessary administrative details (like NI number) for an employer.
- Information relating to private-sector crime or fraud should be supplied only to the proper authorities, and probably only after due process.

M: 'I don't think they should, business and that shouldn't be together like this. Private industry and the public, they should be two separate things'

(Mid, benefits, 45–64)

F: 'I've always assumed that it was confidential, I never gave it a thought that it might not be, but the thought that they might hand out information that, say, electric wheelchair sellers could contact you – that would be a worry'

(Sth, mid-TEA, 45–64)

F: 'If you apply for Housing Benefit when you have a mortgage your mortgage company is told, and I think that's outrageous. Even if it's decided that you're earning too much money and you're not going to get any benefit, your mortgage company still knows that you've applied, and that might jeopardise the future. I think that shouldn't happen at all'

(Lon, benefits, 16–39)

Moreover most participants felt that DSS should not normally be able to get PI *from* the private sector – access to bank and building society records is not thought permissible except in extreme cases (like serious fraud or crime), and then only through legal process.

I: 'How far do you think DSS ought to have access to, say, bank, building society information?'
M: 'Again, none at all'
M: 'Well they'd need a court order wouldn't they?'
F: 'They'd need a court order and you'd need to know about it'

(Mid, low-TEA, 45–64)

---

28 I was focusing on DSS here, but my impression is that the same would hold for government departments in general (and to a large extent the whole public sector).

I: 'Take for example banks, building societies, financial organisations, do you think there is any way in which they should have access to DSS information about individuals under any circumstances?'
M: 'None whatsoever, no never'
I: 'And do you think there's any cases where DSS should have access to information about individuals from banks or anything else?'
M: 'No, no'
F: 'No, definitely not'
M: 'Well it's private sector and Government and the two can't mix'
M: 'Only under certain circumstances, ie court warrants things like that, court order'
I: 'Is that fair enough if they've got a court order?'
M: 'I would imagine they'd have to have some sort of system like that because your major fraudster's then gonna have a bank full of money and nobody's gonna realise where he's got all this money'

(Nth, benefits, 40+)

4.3.5.6 Sharing with the voluntary sector

Most people do not want DSS to share personal information at all with charities and voluntary sector bodies. A minority disagree, because these may be good causes which could benefit the individuals concerned. However, most feel that confidentiality is more important. Moreover people may not want to be bothered – some charities are now seen to pester people. In general charities are thought to have no right to personal information unless it is freely given them by the person concerned.

Advice agencies like CAB might be a partial exception in the voluntary sector. Some would like CAB to have better access to a client's DSS records – but only with the express consent of that individual, they should have no more general rights of access.

M: '(CAB) Their ability to get information on your permission should be expedited, so that if you want information because you're involved in a case for some reason that should be a fast and easy process'

(Mid, graduates, 35–44)

4.3.6 DSS policies and practices

After each scenario participants were usually given a brief account of what DSS views and practices would be. These were often found surprising – they give an impression of an organisation more careful and conscientious about PI disclosure than people expected.

Moreover the surprises were usually pleasant. Although not everyone agreed about all details, people usually felt that the general strategy implied was about right. Many were pleased that their worst fears about widespread and indiscriminate disclosure seemed unfounded.

But there was a good deal of scepticism in many quarters about what they heard – and sometimes rank disbelief, particularly among inner-city participants and some benefit recipients. Some assumed either that the 'policy' was just window-dressing; or that it was a genuine policy, but one not always carried out on the ground.

Scepticism arose partly from general mistrust and cynicism; and partly from a feeling that even if this was a genuine expression of policy, practice on the ground wouldn't match up to it:

- in such a large organisation there are too many managers and staff involved, so it would be hard to control standards
- it is tempting to break the rules – either in the name of 'efficiency', or perhaps even though corruption ('rotten apples', 'money talks').

A few individuals claimed they had actually experienced disclosures which DSS said in the scenarios would not be allowed.

4.3.7 Effects of policy change

It is difficult to assess the practical effects on behaviour if PI is not assumed to be confidential.

To begin with many people already question confidentiality, and often assume it has already begun to break down – probably to a greater extent than it actually has.

Breakdown in confidentiality would make many people more wary about providing information. If you suspect it may be divulged it makes sense to be as economical with it as you can – you would take care to 'think what you're putting down'.

> *M: 'If people haven't got the confidence to go to these people and give them this information they're going to lose confidence in that particular department, and they're going to withhold information that should be brought out into the open. But if they know that it's going to stay in the particular files of that department then they would be more happy to divulge what they should do'*
>
> (Nth, benefits, 60+)

> *M: 'If they start giving out stuff willy-nilly like, people are just not going to give it are they?'*
> *M: 'That's right. I mean where does it stop?'*
> *F: 'Well where would it end? You might as well put a list in your front window for everybody in the road to read or whatever'*
>
> (Mid, low-TEA, 45–64)

Loss of confidentiality also destroys one side of the implicit bargain made. People accept they have to give information they would rather keep to themselves, and in return they expect it to be kept confidential. Some participants felt that if departments and agencies fail to keep their side of the bargain this removes the public's moral obligation to co-operate. They argue that people would then begin to feel morally justified in withholding or perhaps even falsifying information.

> *M: 'I think you've got a principle here, that if you give information, they've got a right to ensure that it's confidential and if you show that they're not treating that information as confidential you don't have to provide them with any more information – and that includes the tax office, whoever it is – if the Government makes the information freely available to everybody then you have no duty then to provide them with any more information'*
>
> (Sth, graduates, 35–44)

> *I: 'If people don't believe that the information they're asking on government forms is going to be confidential, do you think that affects what they do, what they put on the form, whether they fill it in? How they behave?'*
> *F: 'Yeah, definitely. Personal things that they ask, you skip'*
> *F: 'Skip over it wouldn't you, rather than give them the real – '*
> *M: 'I think you might give 'em what you think they'd like to see or what you're happy for them to have, which might not always be the truth'*
>
> (Nth, 16–34)

However, some point out that information is usually given to bodies like DSS under compulsion, and without a lot of discretion or room for manoeuvre. If you don't provide the information you don't get the benefits or services – or you get prosecuted if it is a tax return. There is a powerful folklore that a claim form which is even marginally incomplete will be sent back.

> *M: 'The thing is though you've got to give it, when they ask you for it, you've got to give it, you've got no choice'*
> *M: 'It's not a case of, "Oh well no, I'm not gonna provide that information", so you just leave it blank'*
> *F: 'They'll send it back to ya'*
> *M: 'Because you send it in, you're waiting for a benefit, three weeks later they send it back and say you haven't filled this in'*
> *F: 'You'll come across that same question anyway further on along the form, because it'll be just worded different'*
>
> (Nth, benefits, 40+)

> *M: 'You do what you have to do, you have to follow the system'*
>
> (Mid, benefits, 45–64)

> *M: 'It's a bit of an unfair question because if you refuse to give the information, you'll not get paid'*
> *F: 'You get prosecuted'*
> *M: 'That's right – and I go to the DSS because I need the assistance, so if I need the assistance I've got to be willing to give the information'*
>
> (Mid, low-TEA, 45–64)

Moreover if someone depends on benefits they would probably have to continue to claim willy-nilly, but some suggested that loss of trust could be another factor helping to reduce take-up of benefits. It is inevitably difficult to find specific evidence of this without talking to a special sample of people contemplating a claim, but some effect of this kind seems likely.

> *F: 'I know many old people at the moment, because it's part of my work, will not fill in a form because, "That's my business, it's nothing to do with anybody else", and we've sort of bridged that gap between the time when a man wouldn't tell his wife how much he earned anyway, so that's a sort of age related phobia – and it's still around'*
>
> (Mid, graduates, 35–44)

This seems to be an issue in the NHS context too. Chris Wills writing in the *Health Libraries Review* (1985) says "There is growing concern that confidentiality can be and is being broken, leading to an increasing number of patients/clients who may withhold information which is vital to their treatment or rehabilitation".

On the basis of my conversations, increased information sharing seems more likely to be construed as a negative measure to keep tabs on the citizens than as a positive drive to improve service delivery.

At all events further loss of confidentiality seems likely to damage further both the public's sense of trust in public institutions, and any feeling of reciprocity and mutual respect in their dealings.

Reducing confidentiality also puts a large premium on effective subject access to guard against the risk of transmitting incorrect or misleading information – yet subject access at present seems largely theoretical for most people (see 4.2.5).

ANNEXES

I Methods and sample

II Sample profile

III Recruitment questionnaire

IV Topic guide

V Stimulus material

VI List of sources consulted

VII Letter of authority

ANNEX I METHODS AND SAMPLE

The qualitative study is based on 16 interview sessions (8 group discussions and 8 individual depth interviews, including one couple), involving 69 people from 68 households. The following extracts from recruitment instructions define the method in more detail. The sample profile is in Annex II, and the recruitment questionnaire and letter of authority in Annex III. A more general description of methodology is in Section B.

Extract from recruitment instructions

Introduction

Introduce it as a survey of public attitudes to confidentiality of official information (see questionnaire) being carried out by independent researcher Alan Hedges for the Department of Social Security.

Stress that:

- the survey is confidential, and the names of those taking part will at no stage be reported to the Department of Social Security (or anyone else outside the research team)
- it has no bearing on the benefits people do or might receive
- it is purely a fact-finding project, and there will be no attempt to sell anything to participants as a result of their taking part, or to persuade them to do anything.

People do not need to know anything about the subject or to have particular views about it. There won't be anything difficult about it.

There may be a few things to look at, so please ask anyone who needs **glasses for reading** to bring them with them.

Letter of authority

You will have a letter of authority from DSS to show it is a genuine piece of research.

Numbers per session

The target number per group is 7. I prefer not to work with more than 8 or less than 6. 5 is the minimum acceptable.

Overall requirements

Exclude civil servants working for government departments or agencies, and anyone working in market research.

Session quotas

Quotas for the eight sessions will be as follows:

London	*Group* Mixed TEA Mixed sex Pensioners	*Group* Benefits Mixed sex Aged 16–39	*Depth* Benefits Man 16-29	*Depth* Lone parent Woman 16–29
South	*Group* Graduates Mixed sex Aged 35–44	*Group* Medium TEA Mixed sex Aged 45–64	*Depth* Benefits Man 30–44	*Depth* Benefits Woman 45–64
Midlands	*Group* Early leavers Mixed sex Aged 45-64	*Group* Graduates Mixed sex Aged 35–44	*Depth* Benefits Man 45–64	*Depth* Lone parent Woman 30–44
North	*Group* Mixed TEA Mixed sex Aged 16–34	*Group* Benefits Mixed sex Aged 40+	*Depth* Benefits Man Pensioner	*Depth* Benefits Woman Pensioner

All the groups should be about half men and half women.

Benefits: In groups or depths labelled 'Benefits' everyone must be getting (or have had fairly recent experience of) at least one benefit in either of the following two categories:

Unemployment or means tested benefits: Any of the first four benefits listed above the top line on the questionnaire (2ab) – Income Support, Unemployment Benefit, Family Credit, and/or Housing Benefit.

Sickness or disability benefits: Any of the seven benefits below the bottom line at 2ab – Disability Living Allowance/Attendance Allowance, Disability Working Allowance, Incapacity Benefit/Sickness Benefit, Severe Disablement Allowance, or Industrial Injuries Disablement Benefit.

Note that the three benefits in the middle of the list (Child Benefit, Retirement Pension and One Parent Benefit) *do not* count for the 'benefit' sessions. People getting these will only be eligible for those sessions if they are *also* getting one or more of the benefits listed in categories 1 or 2 above.

Aim for a good mix of different benefits. Ideally about half should be unemployment or means tested, and about half sickness or disability benefits, with a reasonable spread of each.

There should be at least two medically related benefits in the depth interviews.

Note that benefit recipients are sometimes muddled about what they actually do get – but you will largely have to accept what they say at face value. Probe to make sure they have given you *all* their benefits – they may be getting more than one.

There may also be some benefit recipients in the sessions *not* labelled as 'benefits' – just take them as they come. *Anyone* aged 16+ is eligible for these sessions. I would expect something like 2-3 benefit recipients in each of these groups (not more). Out of all 18 people recruited in each area the following numbers should be benefit recipients (as defined above):

- In London and the North aim for about 12–13 on benefits
- In the Midlands and South aim for 6–8 on benefits.

Lone parent: A woman living alone with her child(ren) and getting either Income Support or Family Credit.

TEA (Terminal Education Age): 'Graduates' means people educated to aged 21 or more. 'Early leavers' left school at 16 or earlier. 'Medium TEA' left between 17 and 20.

Working status: In the non-benefit groups, at least half the group should either be in work or have a history of working. This doesn't apply to the benefit groups or depth interviews, where people will probably not be working.

Children: At least half those recruited should have children under 16, except in the pensioner and 45–64 groups.

Timing

The groups will probably last 1½ hours, and depths an hour. But to be safe **leave 1¾ hours between start times for groups, and 1¼ for depth interviews**. Where necessary travel time should be left on top of this.

Groups should be in the evening, although 'pensioner' and 'benefit' groups are likely to be available in the daytime, so these could be afternoon sessions. Depth interviews will mostly be available during the day, and should be fitted round the groups – normally lunchtime, afternoon or early evening.

Venues

Groups in interviewers' homes where possible, providing these are in the right areas, and suitable for the target groups. Otherwise a public venue – hall, pub room or hotel. Somewhere quiet, private and respectable – but not lavish.

Depths can either be in participants' homes (in which case allow travel time, and provide instructions for locating), or in the group venue.

Incentives

Incentives of £15 will be paid to all those taking part. The moderator will provide these.

ANNEX II SAMPLE PROFILE

Sex	
Male	50%
Female	50%
Age	
16–24	10%
25–34	19%
35–39	13%
40–44	21%
45–59	22%
60+	15%
Family composition	
Single person household	28%
Single adult with children under 16	12%
Two adults with children under 16	22%
More than two adults with children under 16	9%
Two adults no children	10%
More than two adults, no children	18%
Whether Benefits (IS, UB, FC, HB and sickness/disability benefits)	
Getting now	55%
Did, not now	4%
Neither	42%
TEA	
Up to 16	52%
17–19	21%
20 or over	27%
SEG	
AB	22%
C1	18%
C2	21%
DE	40%
Working status	
Working full-time	27%
Working part-time	16%
Full-time housewife	13%
Seeking work	14%
Retired	13%
Long-term sick or disabled	16%
Temporarily sick or disabled	2%
Total sample	**68**

Annex III: Recruitment questionnaire

Confidentiality of official information about individuals

Serial number [ ]

We are independent researchers doing a survey for the Department of Social Security about public attitudes to the confidentiality of official information about individual people - what do people think happens to such information, and what do they think ought to happen to it. We would like to invite you to come and give your views.

EXPLAIN ABOUT GROUP DISCUSSION. STRESS THAT THIS WILL JUST BE A FRIENDLY CHAT, AND WILL ITSELF BE CONFIDENTIAL - THE INFORMATION WILL BE USED ONLY FOR RESEARCH PURPOSES, AND NO NAMES OR ADDRESSES WILL BE DISCLOSED

I need to ask you a few questions about yourself and your family now - we have to make sure that we are inviting a proper cross-section of the public.

---

1 Please tell me who lives in your household apart from yourself

Single person household	[ ]	1
Single adult with children under 16	[ ]	2
Two adults with children under 16	[ ]	3
More than two adults with children under 16	[ ]	4
Two adults no children	[ ]	5
More than two adults, no children	[ ]	6

	2a Are you getting any of the benefits on this card now?	2b And are there any other benefits you have had in the fairly recent past?
Income Support	[ ] 01	[ ] 01
Unemployment Benefit	[ ] 02	[ ] 02
Family Credit	[ ] 03	[ ] 03
Housing Benefit	[ ] 04	[ ] 04
One Parent Benefit	[ ] 05	[ ] 05
Child Benefit (Family Allowance)	[ ] 06	[ ] 06
Retirement pension	[ ] 07	[ ] 07
Disability Living Allowance/Attendance Allowance	[ ] 08	[ ] 08
Disability Working Allowance	[ ] 09	[ ] 09
Incapacity Benefit/Sickness Benefit	[ ] 10	[ ] 10
Severe Disablement Allowance	[ ] 11	[ ] 11
Industrial Injuries Disablement Benefit	[ ] 12	[ ] 12

3 How old were you when you finished full time education?

Up to 16 ☐ 1
17-19 ☐ 2
20 or over ☐ 3

Gender

Male ☐ 1
Female ☐ 2

Work status

Working full-time ☐ 1
Working part-time ☐ 2
Full-time housewife ☐ 3
Seeking work ☐ 4
Retired ☐ 5
Long-term sick or disabled ☐ 6
Temporarily sick or disabled ☐ 7

Age

16-24 ☐ 1
25-34 ☐ 2
35-39 ☐ 3
40-44 ☐ 4
45-54 ☐ 5
55-59 ☐ 6
60-64 ☐ 7
65-74 ☐ 8
75+ ☐ 9

Occupation of CWE	**Occupation of respondent (if different)**

SEG

AB ☐ 1
C1 ☐ 2
C2 ☐ 3
DE ☐ 4

Area

Huddersfield ☐ 1
Birmingham ☐ 2
London ☐ 3
Reading ☐ 4

Recruited for Group discussion ☐ 1
Depth interview ☐ 2

Date

Time am/pm

Venue

Name
Address

Telephone

This respondent was recruited face-to-face according to the accompanying instructions and to the Market Research Society Code of Conduct.

Name Signature

Date Duration of interview

Reminder call Attending 1
Unable to attend 2 REPLACE

ANNEX IV TOPIC GUIDE

Topic guide for DSS confidentiality of information study

This guide is a broad menu of issues from which I shall choose relevant topics for individual sessions. There will not be time to look at every question from every angle in every interview. Some of the issues listed are huge, and there is potentially a vast matrix of different types of information which might be used by different players for different purposes – and views about what should happen might well differ from cell to cell of this matrix.

The key focus throughout will be on DSS and its component agencies – but we also need:

- to look at its actual and potential linkages with other government departments, private and public sector bodies and individuals
- to set views about DSS in a comparative context of attitudes to other bodies, both governmental and non-governmental.

The guide is a game-plan not a questionnaire – questions will not usually be asked in this form, and some information will emerge in conversation without direct questioning.

The issues will first be explored broadly and in general terms, then more specifically, using prepared scenarios to ground general notions in particular instances.

A. General interest, concerns

1) How interested or concerned are people about what happens to personal information supplied to:
   DSS or its agencies?
   other government departments?
   other public sector bodies?
   private sector organisations?

2) Are they more concerned about the uses of personal information in the public or private sector? Why?

3) How strong or important are such concerns?

4) Why are people concerned (if they are) – what seem to be the main issues or anxieties in their minds?

5) What sort of picture do people have of the effect of computers and IT on the storage and transmission of data?

6) Do these considerations increase or reduce their concerns? And why? How are they seen to affect the situation?

7) How far are they concerned about generalised confidentiality issues? About specific actions or decisions which might be taken? About the balance of power between the state and the individual?

8) Are they concerned about accuracy or up-to-dateness of information?

B. Assumptions about what currently happens

1) What kinds of information do people think DSS and its agencies actually hold about them (particularly if they are not currently claiming any benefits)?

2) What is believed to happen to the information provided to bodies like BA, CA, CSA through forms and requests for information?
How is it stored, processed, used? Where does it go? Is it on computer or manual records? Does it make any difference to confidentiality?
Who has access to it? What types of people? Levels of staff? For what purposes?
How far is it shared between offices? Between agencies? Outside the Department?
How far is it kept, or destroyed once used?
Who 'owns' the information – DSS who hold and use it, or the individuals who provided it and to whom it relates? Is the 'ownership' of information a meaningful concept?

3) And what about information held by DSS, but not supplied by the individual:
eg records of benefits or contributions paid, claims made, etc.

4) How far are people aware of the restructuring of DSS into agencies? How does this affect confidentiality?

5) Under what circumstances (if at all) would a DSS agency divulge personal information to:
another DSS agency?
another government department or agency?
the police?
other public sector bodies?
commercial/industrial companies?
advice agencies or NGOs?
employers or landlords?
the media?
private individuals?

6) Under what circumstances (if at all) would other bodies divulge personal information to a DSS agency – from:
another DSS agency?
another government department or agency?
the police?
a local authority?

other public sector bodies?
commercial/industrial companies?
advice agencies or NGOs?
charities (eg Motability, caring services?)
employers or landlords?
the media?
private individuals?

7) Are there any safeguards for the confidentiality of personal information? What, and how effective?

8) What picture do they have of computer systems within DSS and its agencies? Do they assume that everyone in the department has access to all computerised information? How is this seen to link between DSS agencies? And between DSS and other Departments, or other bodies?

9) How secure are DSS systems assumed to be? Could people get access to information they weren't supposed to have? Are they worried about data security? What risks do they perceive?

C. What ought to happen

1) What are the perceived advantages and disadvantages of free flows of information:
within government departments?
between government departments/agencies?
between government departments/agencies and other bodies?
local government (eg Housing Benefit, social services)?
the police?
health trusts?
banks and building societies?
commercial/industrial concerns?
charities (eg Motability, caring services?)
employers and landlords?

2) Does it make any difference whether we are talking about case-by case disclosure, or blocks of information?

3) How far are people concerned more with protecting individual privacy and rights, or more with the efficient working of the system? What is the best balance between efficiency and confidentiality? Do we seem to have that now – if not which way should things move?

4) If they are concerned with efficiency, is this more with helping the individual (simplifying information collection, improving service, qualifying for means tested benefits), or with defending the system against unscrupulous individuals (helping to reduce fraud, abuse, crime)?

5) What kinds of personal information should and should not be disclosed? To whom? Under what circumstances?

6) How far should disclosure be made in cases of fraud or crime? To detect actual fraud, or just to reduce the likelihood? Under what safeguards? How happy are people about emergency powers of access, or reserve powers which may not normally be used? Do they trust Departments and Agencies to behave responsibly and fairly?

D. Likely effects of changes in confidentiality rules or practices

1) How would people react and behave if they thought information was more freely transferred or disclosed? Would it affect claiming? What kinds of information would they be concerned about? And disclosed to whom? Or for what purpose?

E. Different kinds of information

1) How far do their views differ between different *types of information* – eg:
Name, address?
Phone number?
NI number?
Identification linked to other information eg addresses:
eg addresses or NI numbers of people in certain categories (with children, getting benefits, got young children)?
Information about partners or family, numbers or ages of children?
Information about employment (where they worked, when changed jobs, etc)?
Information about health, sickness, disability?
Results of medical tests?
Information about income, earnings?
Information about savings, investments?
Information about partner's circumstances – employment, earnings, health?
Information about mortgage, rent, accommodation?
Contributions record?
Benefit history – what currently receiving, or history?

F. Different uses of information

1) How far do their views differ between *uses* of information – eg:
Sharing or keeping information to save having to ask it again?
Cross-checking information to ensure accuracy?
Using for statistical or research purposes in an unidentified way?
Sharing information to detect possible fraud or crime?
Generally helping the authorities to keep tabs on who is doing what?
Building up a detailed picture of each individual across a wide range of information?
Helping to see what other needs individuals might have, what other help they might need?
Co-operating with other agencies trying to help the individual – doctors, social workers, advice agencies etc. ?
Helping commercial organisations to target useful prospects for goods and services?
Debt collection (eg where people default on their landlords)?

G. Different departments/ agencies/ organisations

1) How far do their views differ between *organisations using* information – eg:
The police
Immigration authorities
Tax inspectors, Inland Revenue
Banks, building societies, insurance companies
Credit rating agencies
Employers
Landlords
Social workers, social services departments
CAB, advice agencies
Health authorities, doctors
Media
University researchers, research institutes
Private individuals

H. Protection of confidentiality

1) How far do people feel their needs for and rights to confidentiality of personal information are protected? If so, how?

2) How much protection do they feel they want or need? Do they have enough? If not, in what ways is the situation lacking?

3) Do they differentiate between computer data, manual records, tapes etc?

4) How far are people aware of the DPA?

5) What do they know about it? In particular the provisions about confidentiality and subject access.

6) How far (and in what ways) is it seen to protect confidentiality – and how effectively?

7) How far is it seen to apply to DSS and its agencies? To other government departments?

AMH 30 November 1995

Anticipating that people's repertoire of ideas about the topic would be limited, a range of non-directive stimulus material was devised to help focus thinking the topic. This was mainly used in the second half of the conversation, once spontaneous perceptions had been well ventilated. It was deployed selectively – not all of it was used in every session, and its use depended on the progress of each interview, and on the time available.

The materials comprised:

- lists of:
  - different types of relationship between givers and receivers of information (4.2.1)
  - different types of information. with spaces to write in ratings of their sensitivity (4.2.6)
- 40 specific scenarios detailing possible disclosure situations (4.3.4). These were presented orally, one at a time, sometimes in paraphrased or simplified form. Only a selection were handled in each group.
- a proforma on which people could write for each scenario whether or not they thought the request for information *would* be met by the body concerned – and whether it *should* be met
- a schematic diagram of various bodies who might exchange information (reproduced in 4.3.5, not shown below).

The materials (apart from the item indicated as shown in the report text) are reproduced below in the above order.

Common information, totally shared

Unrestricted access to other database

Freely available on request

Available on request for good reason

Needs special permission

Needs legal process

Not available under any circumstances

Name and address (alone)	
Name and address (linked to other information)	
Phone number (alone)	
Phone number (linked to other information)	
National Insurance number	
National Insurance contributions record	
Whether has children, ages and sexes of children	
Whether a single parent	
Whether married, cohabiting, single, widowed or divorced	
Employment (where they worked, when changed jobs, etc)	
Health, sickness, disability	
Results of medical tests	
Income, earnings	
Savings, investments	
Partner's circumstances – employment, earnings, health	
Whether home is owned or rented	
Amount of mortgage or rent	
Benefit history – what currently getting, or have had in the past	

Charities

6	A school is trying to arrange a reunion for the class of 1970. A member of the school's social committee writes to the DSS and provides a list of names, dates of birth and last known addresses of the class members and asks the DSS for their assistance in locating these people. Should the DSS co-operate?	*This type of request has been received. The DSS would not provide the details requested.*
8	Age Concern/CAB/a private citizen wants to start a pensioners' support group. They write to the DSS and ask for the names and addresses of all pensioners in a particular geographical area. Should the DSS supply the information?	*We have received this type of request. The DSS wouldn't provide this type of information, but we may suggest to the enquirer that they may wish to contact relevant welfare groups within the area.*
31	A CAB advice worker telephones the DSS and asks to discuss Mr X's claim to benefit. Should the DSS discuss Mr X's claim?	*If the office taking the call is convinced that the advice worker is bona fide, then it would be accepted that the person concerned has given implied consent.*

Companies

1	A baby food company writes to the DSS Child Benefit Centre and says that it would like to send a book of complimentary baby care vouchers (worth £25) to all new mothers. The company asks if, on a quarterly basis, it could be provided with a list of the names and addresses of anybody who has made a claim for Child Benefit within the preceding 3 months. Should the DSS provide such a list?	*The DSS wouldn't do this. We have received similar types of requests.*
4	A direct mail catalogue company is trying to trace people who have moved without paying their outstanding debts. The company contacts the DSS and asks for its assistance. Should the DSS co-operate?	*We have received similar requests. The DSS wouldn't provide this type of information unless we were ordered to by a court.*
5	A bank looking to attract new young customers writes to the DSS asking if, on a quarterly basis, it could be provided with the names and addresses of everybody who has been allocated a National Insurance number within the preceding 3 months. Should the DSS co-operate?	*The DSS would not co-operate – we wouldn't provide a bank with these details.*

14	A company redeems life assurance policies from people suffering from terminal illnesses. They buy the policies from the person, eg they pay £20,000 for rights to a policy which may be worth £30,000. The company contacts the DSS and asks them to check their records and let them know if the subjects of the redeemed policies have died, thus enabling them to claim their money. Should the DSS co-operate?	*Although dates of death are ultimately in the public domain, the DSS has no control over when the Registrar of Births Deaths & Marriages makes them public, which can take a considerable time. This request would be better directed to the Registrar.*
15	A life assurance company contacts the DSS asking for the names and addresses of people receiving a terminally ill benefit so that they can make contact and offer their services. Should the DSS co-operate?	*The DSS would not disclose this type of information.*
19	An Electricity Board writes to the DSS asking for their help in locating an occupier who has left their previous address leaving a large unpaid bill. The Electricity Board want the DSS to provide them with the occupier's new address. Should the DSS co-operate?	*The DSS would not co-operate.*
36	A security company wishes to comply with British Standard BSXXXX, which states that all security personnel should have a verifiable employment history for the last ten years. It writes to the DSS and asks for the National Insurance contribution histories for the company's employees. Should the DSS assist the company?	*Information would not be given to the employer, a personal request from the person concerned would be met.*
37	Several large companies approach the DSS requesting a service whereby they can telephone and confirm the National Insurance number an employee has provided. Should the DSS co-operate?	*Information would not be supplied to the employer, a personal request from the person concerned would be met*[1].

Councils

27	A Local Education Authority is willing to let the DSS have access to information it holds on the assessment of students' maintenance grants. The database includes information about the student and his or her parents. Should the DSS be allowed access to this information?	*The DSS would not accept this offer. It is doubtful that the organisations offering the information are legally allowed to do so.*
32	A social worker rings the DSS and says he's dealing with a case of a child at risk. The child's parents have separated. The social worker asks the DSS to provide him with the father's address. Should the DSS co-operate?	*Where a serious welfare need has arisen the DSS would normally co-operate with the social worker.*

1 This was the statement originally supplied by DSS. After the fieldwork was finished it emerged that NI numbers can in fact be *verified* to employers.

DSS

28	A National Insurance Inspector, on a routine visit to a local factory, finds the tax and NI affairs of the company in good order. However, as a precaution he takes a copy of the company's payroll and passes it to a colleague in the Benefits Agency to see if there is possibly any benefit fraud. Should he do this?	*The passing on of information would be in order only if the Inspector had reasonable grounds for suspecting fraud. "Fishing expeditions" are not acceptable.*

29	The Benefits Agency asks the Child Support Agency to provide them with the details of any absent parent who has a new partner. The BA want the CSA to provide them with a list detailing both the absent parent's and the new partner's, name, address, and NI no. The BA say that this will help them to reduce possible "single parent fraud" (ie the new partners may be single parent benefits).	*The passing on of information would be in order only if the BA had reasonable grounds for suspecting fraud. "Fishing expeditions" are not acceptable.*

34	The Child Support Agency ask Benefits Agency for the amount of benefit being paid to an absent parent who is receiving Incapacity Benefit. Can it be given?	*Information held by the Secretary of State in connection with the Benefits Acts can be used for the purposes of the Child Support Acts.*

Employer

25	An employer rings the DSS. A considerable amount of cash has gone missing, and one of their employees has disappeared. The employer asks if the DSS can help trace the employee. Should the DSS help?	*Although information can be disclosed to aid the apprehension or prosecution of an offender, there is no proof that the person concerned is guilty. The DSS would not therefore disclose any information.*
26	A large corporation (eg a company like BT or British Gas) has contacted the DSS and offered it access to payroll records so that it can see if any of the company's employees are working whilst claiming benefit. Should the DSS accept the offer?	*The DSS would not accept this offer. It is doubtful that the organisations offering the information are legally allowed to do so.*

Government

12	The Lord Chancellor's Department contacts the DSS asking for help with the tracing of fine defaulters. Should the DSS assist them by providing addresses?	*The DSS would not normally provide this type of information.*
13	The Foreign and Commonwealth Office (F&CO) contact the DSS to confirm the whereabouts of Mr X and whether he is in receipt of benefit. Mr X has failed to repay a repatriation grant, this is where a British national abroad approaches a British Embassy asking to be repatriated back to the UK. Receipt of benefit may affect any recovery action F&CO consider. Should the DSS provide the F&CO with the information requested?	*The DSS would not normally provide this type of information.*

21	DSS asks the Inland Revenue for up-to-date information on all tax-payers in order to confirm that tax declarations are consistent with information on benefit claims. Should the Inland Revenue co-operate with the DSS?	*The transfer would be lawful but the Inland Revenue feels it would be against a long tradition of confidentiality in tax affairs. It also believes it could lead to people falsifying tax returns.*

24	The Ministry of Defence want to provide the DSS with a list of service personnel who have gone absent without leave. Should the DSS accept this list and should they give the military the latest address of anyone on the list who makes a claim for benefit?	*No such offer has been received – If it were the DSS would need to assess the seriousness of the offence before deciding if any information could be disclosed to the MoD.*

30	The Family Credit unit (Family Credit is an in-work means tested benefit) are concerned that some of the earnings declarations made by their clients may be incorrect. They therefore contact the Inland Revenue and ask them to check the earnings declaration against the tax/earnings records that they hold. Should the DSS seek the Inland Revenues assistance?	*The DSS do not do this. If the DSS wishes to verify earnings it will normally write to the customer and ask for sight of wage slips.*
35	The Ministry of Defence wants to monitor the levels of unemployment among ex-service personnel. They want to provide the DSS with blocks of National Insurance numbers which will represent various categories of service-men eg service, rank, age, trade etc. The DSS would then check the National Insurance numbers and provide a statistical response eg X% of category Y registered as unemployed at 3,6, & 12 months after leaving the service. Should the DSS co-operate?	*As the information is anonymised and does not identify any particular person, it could be provided.*
38	The Immigration Department approaches the DSS and asks for its assistance in tracing illegal immigrants. The names of the illegal immigrants are not necessarily known, or they may be using false names, and the DSS will therefore have to search its files for other clues. Should the DSS co-operate? Note: Most illegal immigrants are white and come from Eastern European countries.	*DSS will co-operate but only on a case by case basis and not in bulk.*

Individuals

7	Mr X is trying to trace Mr Y. In 1980 Mr X took Mr Y to court and Mr Y was ordered to pay compensation to Mr X. Mr Y failed to pay any compensation and left the country. Mr X believes that Mr Y has now returned to this country. Should the DSS assist Mr X?	*We have received similar requests. The DSS wouldn't provide Mr X with this type of information unless we were ordered to by a court.*

9	A constituent complains to her MP that she has reported a case of fraud to the DSS but that no action appears to have been taken. The MP writes to the DSS asking to be kept informed of the progress of enquiries and the outcome of any investigation. What should the DSS do?	*The DSS would decline the MP's request.*
10	The parents of a 17 year old girl who has run away from her home in the North of England asks the DSS for the address of their daughter who they believe has settled in the King's Cross area of London. The parents know the reputation of the area and are worried about their daughter's moral welfare. The daughter claims to have been sexually abused at home by her father and is in receipt of benefit. She has expressly requested that her address should not be given to her parents. The DSS thinks she stands little chance of getting work and would be better off at home where she would have to be maintained by her parents. What should the DSS do?	*The DSS would not disclose the daughter's address.*

11	An angry father demands to know the whereabouts of his son, in respect of whom he has been granted access rights by the Courts. He is unwilling to make child support payments to the DSS unless he is able to exercise his right of access to his son. DSS records show the man has a history of violence toward his former partner though not toward his son. What should the DSS do?	*This does happen – more or less. The DSS would not disclose the child's whereabouts and would continue to pursue our request for child support payments.*
18	Someone is at the centre of a controversy for reasons that are not in any way connected with social security. However, the person concerned has no visible means of support and there are rumours circulating that they are in receipt of benefit. The DSS is asked to confirm or deny these rumours. The person is in receipt of benefit. What should the DSS do?	*DSS would neither confirm nor deny receipt – if DSS denied receipt when appropriate it would soon become apparent that the absence of denial meant confirmation.*
20	A solicitor acting for a parent with care, who is in receipt of child support maintenance, asks the CSA for the absent parent's address, which is needed in connection with parent with care's divorce proceedings. Should the CSA give it?	*The DSS would not provide this information unless it was compelled to by law or ordered to by a court.*

33	A parent with care queries the amount of her maintenance assessment, which has been reduced because protected income applies (this is the minimum amount that the absent parent needs to support their "new" family). Can she be told the absent parent's net family income when this contains income belonging to the absent parent's new partner?	*Regulation 10 of the Child Support Maintenance Assessment Procedure Regulations allow for the maintenance assessment notification form to contain this information, so the parent with care should have received it already. Regulation 9A of the Child Support Information Evidence and Disclosure Regulations would allow for the disclosure – essential information needed to explain the maintenance assessment.*
39	A solicitor is trying to locate a beneficiary under a will, who stands to inherit £100,000. She has made several unsuccessful attempts to find the individual via various privately run tracing agencies. The solicitor writes to the DSS and asks for their help. She provides the beneficiary's name, maiden name, date of birth and last known address. Should the DSS assist the solicitor?	*The DSS operates a letter forwarding service in cases of family crisis or where there is benefit to the person concerned. This service would be appropriate in this case.*
40	A woman writes to the DSS saying that she is trying to trace a sister that she has not seen for many years. She says that they lost contact because her sister was adopted; or because her sister ran away from home or just because of the passing of time. The woman says that she needs to contact her sister because she may have a hereditary disorder which has only recently come to light and of which she needs to be informed. Should the DSS help trace the sister?	*The DSS would not disclose the sister's address to the enquirer, but the letter forwarding service may be appropriate in this case.*

Landlords

2	A landlord contacts a DSS office and complains that his tenant who was on income support and housing benefit has absconded without paying four weeks rent. The landlord wants the DSS to provide him with his ex-tenant's new address so that he can ask his solicitor to pursue the arrears. Should the DSS provide the landlord with the new address?	*We have received these types of requests. The DSS wouldn't provide a landlord with this type of information unless we were ordered to by a court.*

3	A group of young lads have left their former address owing rent arrears and having vandalised the property. They have moved to a squat. Their former landlord feels sure that they will be in receipt of benefit, if not now then sometime in the future, and asks to be told of their whereabouts. The landlord is willing to indemnify the DSS against any legal action for breach of confidence. Should the DSS co-operate?	*Requests of this nature have been received. DSS would not provide any information to the former landlord but the question of indemnity has not yet arisen. The necessary information would be given on the order of a court.*

Media

17	The DSS is criticised in the Press for paying benefit to what is popularly viewed as a particularly undeserving case. The claimant has admitted being in receipt of benefit and has given permission for their case to be discussed with a newspaper reporter. The DSS can only defend itself by revealing other facts that have not yet been reported on. What should the DSS do?	*As a matter of policy DSS will not discuss details of an individual case with the press even with consent of the person concerned.*

Police

22	A police sergeant contacts a local DSS office. He says that he is investigating a drug trafficking offence and that he needs to speak to Mr X. Should the office give the sergeant the address of Mr X?	*Due to the seriousness of the crime the DSS would assist.*
23	A police inspector writes to a DSS office, and states that he is trying to trace Mr X who has been charged with shoplifting and failed to make a court appearance. Should the office provide the inspector with the address of Mr X?	*DSS would not assist as shoplifting is not considered to be a serious crime.*

Research

16	A researcher writes to the DSS and asks if they could check their records and provide him with the names and addresses of any surviving first world war veterans, so that he can interview them and record their memories for posterity. The researcher says that the profit from any publication would be paid over to ex service organisations or 15% of the profit from any publication would be paid to ex-service organisations.	*We have received this type of request. The DSS wouldn't provide this type of information, but we may suggest to the enquirer that they may wish to contact relevant welfare groups.*

Number	**Would** they agree?			**Should** they agree?		
	Would	?	Wouldn't	Should	?	Shouldn't
	Would	?	Wouldn't	Should	?	Shouldn't
	Would	?	Wouldn't	Should	?	Shouldn't
	Would	?	Wouldn't	Should	?	Shouldn't
	Would	?	Wouldn't	Should	?	Shouldn't
	Would	?	Wouldn't	Should	?	Shouldn't
	Would	?	Wouldn't	Should	?	Shouldn't
	Would	?	Wouldn't	Should	?	Shouldn't
	Would	?	Wouldn't	Should	?	Shouldn't
	Would	?	Wouldn't	Should	?	Shouldn't
	Would	?	Wouldn't	Should	?	Shouldn't
	Would	?	Wouldn't	Should	?	Shouldn't
	Would	?	Wouldn't	Should	?	Shouldn't
	Would	?	Wouldn't	Should	?	Shouldn't
	Would	?	Wouldn't	Should	?	Shouldn't
	Would	?	Wouldn't	Should	?	Shouldn't
	Would	?	Wouldn't	Should	?	Shouldn't
	Would	?	Wouldn't	Should	?	Shouldn't
	Would	?	Wouldn't	Should	?	Shouldn't
	Would	?	Wouldn't	Should	?	Shouldn't
	Would	?	Wouldn't	Should	?	Shouldn't
	Would	?	Wouldn't	Should	?	Shouldn't
	Would	?	Wouldn't	Should	?	Shouldn't
	Would	?	Wouldn't	Should	?	Shouldn't
	Would	?	Wouldn't	Should	?	Shouldn't
	Would	?	Wouldn't	Should	?	Shouldn't
	Would	?	Wouldn't	Should	?	Shouldn't
	Would	?	Wouldn't	Should	?	Shouldn't
	Would	?	Wouldn't	Should	?	Shouldn't
	Would	?	Wouldn't	Should	?	Shouldn't
	Would	?	Wouldn't	Should	?	Shouldn't
	Would	?	Wouldn't	Should	?	Shouldn't
	Would	?	Wouldn't	Should	?	Shouldn't
	Would	?	Wouldn't	Should	?	Shouldn't
	Would	?	Wouldn't	Should	?	Shouldn't
	Would	?	Wouldn't	Should	?	Shouldn't
	Would	?	Wouldn't	Should	?	Shouldn't
	Would	?	Wouldn't	Should	?	Shouldn't

ANNEX VI LIST OF SOURCES CONSULTED

The research was preceded by a literature review. This was not exhaustive – a quick trawl for relevant material rather than a definitive search. The main purposes were

- to see whether there was evidence already available which could answer some of the problems
- to help develop thinking about the project.

I used a variety of sources and on-line databases, including:

- LSE Library (catalogues, microfiches etc)
- British Library (Science Reference And Information Section)
- Sociofile
- Datastar
- SIGLE (Grey paper index)
- World Wide Web (a brief trawl of a few key search engines)
- HMSO catalogues
- Catalogue of British Official Publications (non-HMSO) (1990-1995).

I did keyword database and catalogue searches using combinations of words like 'confidentiality', 'data', 'privacy', 'data protection', 'computers', 'database' etc.

I found:

- a lot of material on both the legal and the computer-technical aspects of data protection, which was not exhaustively scanned, since it usually proved at best only peripherally relevent to the subject in hand
- some material on the use of PI for research purposes, again usually only peripherally relevant
- a lot of old sources, dating from the run-up to the 1984 Data Protection Act, and its immediate aftermath
- very little direct research evidence about public perceptions and attitudes (apart from a few studies kindly made available by the DPR).

Main sources:

10th and 11th reports of the Data Protection Registrar DPR, HMSO, 1994 and 1995

Confidentiality and the Data Protection Act Chris Wills, Asst Director of Nursing Services (Community), Ealing Health Authority, Health Libraries Review, 1985,2, p188

Computer security and privacy abstracts Techgnosis, Manchester 1989

Data Protection and Security for personal computers Robert Schifreen, Oxford Elsevier Advanced Technology 1992

Data Protection Codes of Practice National Computing Centre, Blackwell 1990

Data Protection Act Guidelines (3rd Series, 1984) Office of the Data Protection Registrar, 1994

Data Protection in Health Information Systems: Where Do We Stand? Griesser, Jardel, Kenny & Sauter, North-Holland, 1983, ISBN: 0-444-86713-9

DHA use of FPC patient registration data (consultation document) DHSS 1987

Government and Information Patrick Birkinshaw, Butterworth 1990

Introduction to Data Protection in the NHS DOH 1994

Personal Data Protection in Health and Social Services (Penelope Pearce *et al*, Croom Helm 1988

Personal Information: Privacy and the Law Raymond Wacks, OUP, (1989), ISBN: 0-19-825867-4

Privacy and Data Protection, an international bibliography ed David Flaherty, Mansell 1984

Privacy and Human Rights James Michael, Unesco/Dartmouth Publishing, 1994, ISBN: 92-3-102808-1

Private Lives and Public Policies Duncan, Jabire and de Wolf, US Panel On Confidentiality And Data Access, Executive Summary, National Academy Press, 1993

Regulating Privacy: Data Protection Policy in Europe and the United States Colin J Bennett, Cornell University Press, 1992, ISBN: 0-8014-8010-8

The Data Protection Act of 1984: A qualitative study Alan Hedges 1987, unpublished report on research for COI and the Data Protection Registrar

The general public's atitude to providing information to the DSS/Benefits Agency and the DVLA One World Research & Communications, unpublished debrief notes on research for COI and the Data Protection Registrar, April '93

ANNEX VII LETTER OF AUTHORITY

Below is the text of the DSS letter of authority for the research.

Ref: ATM 4064/JN 604

Dear Sir/Madam

CONFIDENTIALITY OF OFFICIAL INFORMATION

This letter is to confirm that the Department of Social Security (DSS) has asked independent researcher Alan Hedges to carry out a survey of public attitudes to the confidentiality of information supplied to DSS, other government departments and to other official bodies.

We want to find out what the public thinks should happen to safeguard information about individuals. We need to know this as a basis for future planning and policy.

The survey will be simple and informal, and entirely confidential. Those who take part will not be identified to DSS or to any other body.

If you would like to know more about the survey or have any queries, you can telephone me on 0171 962 8271.

We hope that you will agree to take part. Thank you very much for your help.

Yours sincerely

Andrea Garman
Social Research Branch

OTHER RESEARCH REPORTS AVAILABLE:

No.	*Title*	*ISBN*	*Price*
1.	Thirty Families: Their living standards in unemployment	0 11 761683 4	£6.65
2.	Disability, household income & expenditure	0 11 761755 5	£5.65
3.	Housing Benefit Reviews	0 11 761821 7	£16.50
4.	Social Security & Community Care: The case of the Invalid Care Allowance	0 11 761820 9	£9.70
5.	The Attendance Allowance Medical Examination: Monitoring consumer views	0 11 761819 5	£5.50
6.	Lone Parent Families in the UK	0 11 761868 3	£12.75
7.	Incomes In and Out of Work	0 11 761910 8	£17.20
8.	Working the Social Fund	0 11 761952 3	£9.00
9.	Evaluating the Social Fund	0 11 761953 1	£22.00
10.	Benefits Agency National Customer Survey 1991	0 11 761956 6	£16.00
11.	Customer Perceptions of Resettlement Units	0 11 761976 6	£13.75
12.	Survey of Admissions to London Resettlement Units	0 11 761977 9	£8.00
13.	Researching the Disability Working Allowance Self Assessment Form	0 11 761834 9	£7.25
14.	Child Support Unit National Client Survey 1992	0 11 762060 2	£30.00
15.	Preparing for Council Tax Benefit	0 11 762061 0	£5.65
16.	Contributions Agency Customer Satisfaction Survey 1992	0 11 762064 5	£18.00
17.	Employers' Choice of Pension Schemes: report of a qualitative study	0 11 762073 4	£5.00
18.	GPs and IVB: A qualitative study of the role of GPs in the award of Invalidity Benefit	0 11 762077 7	£12.00
19.	Invalidity Benefit: A Survey of Recipients	0 11 762087 4	£10.75

20.	Invalidity Benefit: A Longitudinal Survey of New Recipients	0 11 762088 2	£19.95
21.	Support for Children: A comparison of arrangements in fifteen countries	0 11 762089 0	£22.95
22.	Pension Choices: A survey on personal pensions in comparison with other pension options	0 11 762091 2	£18.95
23.	Crossing National Frontiers	0 11 762131 5	£17.75
24.	Statutory Sick Pay	0 11 762147 1	£23.75
25.	Lone Parents and Work	0 11 762148 x	£12.95
26.	The Effects of Benefit on Housing Decisions	0 11 762157 9	£18.50
27.	Making a Claim for Disability Benefits	0 11 762162 5	£12.95
28.	Contributions Agency Customer Satisfaction Survey 1993	0 11 762220 6	£20.00
29.	Child Support Agency National Client Satisfaction Survey 1993	0 11 762224 9	£33.00
30.	Lone Mothers	0 11 762228 1	£16.75
31.	Educating Employers	0 11 762249 4	£8.50
32.	Employers and Family Credit	0 11 762272 9	£13.50
33.	Direct Payments from Income Support	0 11 762290 7	£16.50
34.	Incomes and Living Standards of Older People	0 11 762299 0	£24.95
35.	Choosing Advice on Benefits	0 11 762316 4	£13.95
36.	First-time Customers	0 11 762317 2	£25.00
37.	Contributions Agency Customer Satisfaction Survey 1994	0 11 762339 3	£21.00
38.	Managing Money in Later Life	0 11 762340 7	£22.00
39.	Child Support Agency National Client Satisfaction Survey 1994	0 11 762341 5	£35.00
40.	Changes in Lone Parenthood	0 11 762349 0	£20.00
41.	Evaluation of Disability Living Allowance and Attendance Allowance	0 11 762351 2	£40.00
42.	War Pensions Agency Customer Satisfaction Survey 1994	0 11 762358 X	£18.00

43.	Paying for Rented Housing	0 11 762370 9	£19.00
44.	Resettlement Agency Customer Satisfaction Survey 1994	0 11 762371 7	£16.00
45.	Changing Lives and the Role of Income Support	0 11 762405 5	£20.00
46.	Social Assistance in OECD Countries: Synthesis Report	0 11 762407 1	£22.00
47.	Social Assistance in OECD Countries: Country Report	0 11 762408 X	£47.00
48.	Leaving Family Credit	0 11 762411 X	£18.00
49.	Women and Pensions	0 11 762422 5	£35.00
50.	Pensions and Divorce	0 11 762423 5	£25.00
51.	Child Support Agency Client Satisfaction Survey 1995	0 11 762424 1	£22.00
52.	Take Up of Second Adult Rebate	0 11 762390 3	£17.00
53.	Moving off Income Support	0 11 7623946	£26.00
	Social Security Research Yearbook 1990–91	0 11 761747 4	£8.00
	Social Security Research Yearbook 1991–92	0 11 761833 0	£12.00
	Social Security Research Yearbook 1992–93	0 11 762150 1	£13.75
	Social Security Research Yearbook 1993–94	0 11 762302 4	£16.50
	Social Security Research Yearbook 1994–95	0 11 762362 8	£20.00

Further information regarding the content of the above may be obtained from:

Department of Social Security
Attn. Keith Watson
Social Research Branch
Analytical Services Division 5
10th Floor, Adelphi
1–11 John Adam Street
London WC2N 6HT
Telephone: 0171 962 8557

Printed in the UK for The Stationery Office
Dd303110 11/96 C11 G3397 10170

Published by The Stationery Office and available from:

The Publications Centre
(mail, telephone and fax orders only)
PO Box 276, London SW8 5DT
General enquiries 0171 873 0011
Telephone orders 0171 873 9090
Fax orders 0171 873 8200

The Stationery Office Bookshops
49 High Holborn, London WC1V 6HB
(counter service and fax orders only)
Fax 0171 831 1326
68-69 Bull Street, Birmingham B4 6AD
0121 236 9696 Fax 0121 236 9699
33 Wine Street, Bristol BS1 2BQ
0117 926 4306 Fax 0117 929 4515
9-21 Princess Street, Manchester M60 8AS
0161 834 7201 Fax 0161 833 0634
16 Arthur Street, Belfast BT1 4GD
01232 238451 Fax 01232 235401
The Stationery Office Oriel Bookshop
The Friary, Cardiff CF1 4AA
01222 395548 Fax 01222 384347
71 Lothian Road, Edinburgh EH3 9AZ
(counter service only)

Customers in Scotland may
mail, telephone or fax their orders to:
Scottish Publications Sales
South Gyle Crescent, Edinburgh EH12 9EB
0131 479 3141 Fax 0131 479 3142

Accredited Agents
(see Yellow Pages)

and through good booksellers